CW00665119

Richard Morris

The Buddhavamsa and the Cariya-Pitaka

Vol. I

Richard Morris

The Buddhavamsa and the Cariya-Pitaka
Vol. I

ISBN/EAN: 9783348014670

Printed in Europe, USA, Canada, Australia, Japan

Cover: Foto ©Lupo / pixelio.de

More available books at **www.hansebooks.com**

Pali Text Society.

THE

BUDDHAVAṂSA

AND THE

CARIYÂ-PIṬAKA.

EDITED BY

THE REV. RICHARD MORRIS, M.A., LL.D.,

EX-PRESIDENT OF THE PHILOLOGICAL SOCIETY.

PART I.—TEXT.

LONDON:

PUBLISHED FOR THE PALI TEXT SOCIETY,

BY HENRY FROWDE,

OXFORD UNIVERSITY PRESS WAREHOUSE, 7, PATERNOSTER ROW.

1882.

HERTFORD:
PRINTED BY STEPHEN AUSTIN AND SONS.

TO

SUBHÛTI UNNÂNSÊ,

OF WASKAḌUWA,

THE LEARNED EDITOR OF THE "ABHIDHÂNA-PPADÎPIKÂ," AND AUTHOR OF THE "NÂMA-MÂLÂ,"

IN GRATEFUL ACKNOWLEDGMENT OF THE GENEROUS AID HE HAS RENDERED TO EUROPEAN SCHOLARS, AND IN SINCERE RESPECT FOR HIS ENLIGHTENED SCHOLARSHIP

THIS LITTLE WORK IS

DEDICATED.

PREFACE.

THE BUDDHAVAṂSA.

In preparing the present text of the Buddhavaṃsa I have made use of the following manuscripts:

1. The Phayre MS., written in Burmese character, in the India Office Library.

2. The Wilson MS. (Burmese character) in the Bodleian Library, Oxford.

3. A MS. on paper, with various readings from two other MSS., transliterated from copies in Siṅhalese writing by Dewa Aranolis. It was formerly in the possession of Dr. Rhys Davids, but is now in the University Library, Cambridge.

4. An imperfect MS. in my own collection in Siṅhalese character.

5–7. A copy of the Madhurattha-vilâsinî, a commentary on the Buddhavaṃsa, presented to me by Subhuti, the learned author of the Nâmamâlâ. As the commentary repeats the greater part of the text, it has been very helpful in checking the variations of the various manuscripts.

I propose in Part II. to give various readings and extracts from the commentary.

The Buddhavaṃsa gives the history of the twenty-four Buddhas who preceded Gotama-Buddha during the last twelve world-cycles (kappas). They are as follows:—Dîpaṅkara, Koṇḍañña, Maṅgala, Sumana, Revata, Sobhita, Anomadassi, Paduma, Nârada, Padumuttara, Sumedha, Sujâta, Piyadassi, Atthadassi, Dhammadassi, Siddhattha, Tissa, Phussa, Vipassi, Sikhi, Vessabhu, Kakusandha, Koṇâgamana, Kassapa.

Then follows Gotama; after him will come Metteyya.

The four Nikâyas make no mention of twenty-four Buddhas. In the Dîghanikâya only *six* of them are enumerated:

Vipassi, Sikhi, Vessabhu, Kakusandha, Koṇâgamana, and Kassapa. We find these names in two discourses: the Mahâpadhâna-sutta and the Âtanâṭiya-sutta. In the "Catena of Buddhist Scriptures from the Chinese," p. 159, we find these six Buddhas, in the order already mentioned, in a work which Mr. Beal designates as the Pâtimokkha.[1]

I have also found in the Mâratajjaniya-sutta of the Majjhima-nikâya a reference to Kakusandha and his pupil Sañjîva.

In the Aruṇavatisutta (in the Paritta) mention is made of Sikhi and his two agga-sâvakas Abhibhu and Sambhava.

The Mahâpadhâna-sutta contains the history of Vipassi, but the legends connected with his name are identical with those related of Gotama in the Buddhavaṃsa.

Dr. Oldenberg thinks that such stories were not originally a part of Gotama's history, but were transferred from the older Buddhas to the last, in order to add lustre to their successor Gotamabuddha.

The Buddhavaṃsa may be a mere poetical expansion of some short prose history of the Buddhas who appeared before Gotama's time.

The Northern Buddhists had also Buddha-histories. The Mahâvastu has a long list of Buddhas (see Senart's edition, pp. 110–120, 136–139), and gives a detailed account of Dîpaṅkara (p. 193) and Maṅgala (p. 249).

Professor Beal has translated the legend of Dîpaṅkara-Buddha from the Chinese *Fu-pen-hing-tsi-king* (Miscellaneous Notices respecting the Birth and History of Buddha), translated by Ajñânakûṭa, a native of Gandhâra, in Northern India, who lived in the time of the Tsui dynasty (581–617 A.D.). In his "Romantic History of Sakya-Buddha" Mr. Beal calls this Chinese work a translation of the *Abhinishkramanasûtra*.

The Chinese life of Dîpaṅkara agrees in most particulars with that in the Mahâvastu, and not with the history of this Buddha as contained in the Pâli Buddhavaṃsa. In both, too, *Megha* takes the place of *Sumedha* in the Southern version.

We have hardly sufficient material before us for har-

[1] The *Svayambhû Purâṇa* also gives these six buddhas in the same order. (*The Sanskrit Buddhist Literature of Nepal*, by Râjendralâla Mitra, p. 249).

monizing the Northern and Southern lists of the Buddhas. The following belong to both divisions: Dîpañkara, Koṇḍañña, Maṅgala, Padumuttara, Piyadassi, Atthadassi, Tissa, Phussa, Vipassi, Sikhi, Vessabhu, Kakusandha, Koṇâgamana, Kassapa. Probably Sarvâdhibhu corresponds to Anuttara just as Devaṣruta seems to be another name for Vessabhu. It seems quite safe however to connect the Chinese *Kanakamuni* with *Kanakaparvata* in the Mahâvastu and with the Pâli *Koṇâgamana*. The commentary to the Buddhavaṃsa states that Koṇâgamana stands for *Kanaka-gamana*, "for at the instant of his birth throughout Jambudîpa a golden shower descended;" and according to the text of the Buddhavaṃsa Gotama was at that time the monarch PABBATA, so that Kanaka-gamana may have been known as Kanaka, Kanakamuni, Kanaka-pabbata, etc.

The three immediate predecessors of Gotama were Brâhmans, and seem to be mentioned with especial honour.

The bowl in which Gotama received the alms of Sujâtâ descended into the lake of the Nâga King, Mahâkâlana, where it remained surmounting the bowls of the three former Buddhas (Hardy, M.B., p. 192; Alabaster's Wheel of the Law, p. 146).

These Buddhas were held in great reverence not only in India, but also in Burmah (Hardy, M.B. pp. 88, 89). According to Chinese authorities, the systems of Kakusandha, Koṇâgamana, and Kassapa were firmly established for ages, while those of the three Buddhas who preceded them lasted but for a short time.

These three (Vipassi, Sikhi, and Vessabhu) "did not extensively declare their law for the sake of their followers, and did not bind their rules as a code, did not deliver the Pratimoksha; and so, after their Nirvâna, their disciples, through lack of discipline, were scattered and demoralized: . . . . ." (Beal's *Abstract of Four Lectures on Buddhist Literature in China*, p. 54.)

The Commentary to the *Buddhavaṃsa* furnishes us with some interesting particulars respecting the composition of the text. I here give the original Pâli with Turnour's translation.

Kenâyaṃ desito kattha kass' atthâya ca desito kimatthâya kadâ kassa vacanaṃ kena câbhato?

Sabbaṃ etaṃ vidhiṃ vatvâ pubbam eva samâsato pacchâhaṃ buddhavaṃsassa karissâma atthavaṇṇanan ti.

Tattha kenâyam desito ti? Ayaṃ buddhavaṃso kena desito? Sabbadhammesu appaṭihatañâṇâcârena dasabalena catuvesârajjavisarâdena dhammarâjena dhammasâminâ Tathâgatena sabbaññunâ sammâsambuddhena desito.

Kattha desito ti? Kapilavatthumahânagare Nigrodhamahâvihâre paramaruciradassanadevamanussasannipâtabhûte ratanacaṅkame caṅkamantena desito.

Kassatthâya ca desito ti? Dvâsîtiyâ ñâtisahassânaṃ anekakoṭinañ ca devamanussânam atthâya desito. Kimatthaya desito ti? Catur' oghanittharaṇatthâya?

Kadâ desito ti? Bhagavâ pathamabodhiyaṃ vîsativassâni anibaddhavâso hutvâ yattha yattha phâsu hoti tattha tatth' eva gantvâ vasi. Kathaṃ paṭhamavassam? Isipatane dhammacakkappavattetvâ aṭṭhârasabrahmakoṭiyo amatapânaṃ pâyetvâ Bârâṇasiyaṃ upanissâya Isipatane Migadâye vasi: dutiya-

---

By whom was this *Buddhavaṃsa* propounded? Where, on whose or what account, and when was it delivered? Whose discourse is it, and how has it been perpetuated?

In the first instance, concisely explaining all these points, I shall then enter upon a detailed commentary on the *Buddhavaṃsa*.

By whom was this *Buddhavaṃsa* propounded? It was propounded by the supreme Buddha who had acquired an infallible knowledge of all the *dhammâ*, who was gifted with the ten powers, who had achieved the four *vessarajjâni*, was the *râja* of *dhamma*, the lord of justice, the omniscient Tathagata.

Where did he propound it? He propounded it at the great city *Kapilavatthu*, at the great *Nigrodhavihâra*, in the act of perambulating in the *ratanacaṅkama*, which attracted the gaze of gods and of men by its pre-eminent and exquisite beauty.

On whose account? He propounded it for the benefit of twenty-two thousand kinsmen and of innumerable *kotiyas* of men and gods.

On what account? He propounded it that he might rescue them from the four *oghas* (torrents of the passions).

Where did he propound it? Bhagavâ during the first twenty years of his Buddhahood led a houseless life (of a pilgrim) sojourning at such places as he found most convenient to dwell in, viz. out of regard for *Bârânasi* he tarried the first year at the *Isipatana*, an edifice (in that city) near which no living creature could be vassaṃ Râjagahaṃ upanissâya Veluvanamahâvihâre: tatiyacatuṭṭhâni pi tatth' eva: pañcamaṃ Vesâliyaṃ upanissâya mahâvane Kuṭâgârasâlâyaṃ: chatthamaṃ Maṅkulapabbate: sattamaṃ Tâvatiṃsabhavane: aṭṭhamaṃ Bhagge Suṃsumâragiriṃ nissâya Bhesakalâvane: navamaṃ Kosambiyaṃ: dasamaṃ Pârileyyake vanasaṇḍe: ekâdasamaṃ Nâlâya Brâhmaṇagâme: dvâdasamaṃ Verañjâya: terasamaṃ Câliyapabbate: cuddasamaṃ Jetavanamahâvihâre: pañcadasamaṃ Kapilavatthumahânagare: solasamaṃ Âḷavakaṃ dametvâ caturâsîtiyâ pâṇasahassâni amatapânaṃ pâyetvâ Aḷaviyaṃ: sattarasamaṃ Râjagahe yeva; attharasamaṃ Câliyapabbate yeva tathâ: ekûnavîsatimaṃ pana vassaṃ Râjagahe yeva vasi: tena vuttaṃ Bhagavâ hi pathamabodhiyaṃ vîsativassâni anibaddhavâso hutvâ yattha yattha phâsukaṃ hoti tattha tatth' eva gantvâ vasîti.

Tato patthâya pana Sâvaṭṭhiyaṃ yeva upanissâya Jetavanamahâvihâre ca Pubbârâme ca dhuvapari[bho]gavasena vasi:

Yadâ pana satthâ Buddho hutvâ Bârâṇasiyaṃ Isipaṭane

---

deprived of life,—establishing the supremacy of his faith and administering to eighteen *kotiyas* of Brahmas the heavenly draught (*nibbâna*). The second year he dwelt at the *Veluvanamahâvihâra* in *Râjagaha*, for the spiritual welfare of that city. The third and fourth years he continued at the same place. The fifth year, out of consideration for *Vesâli*, he dwelt in the *Kûtâgâra* hall in the *Mahâvanavihâra* near that city. The sixth at the *Makula* mountain. The seventh at *Tâvatiṃsabhavana* (one of the devalokas). The eighth year, for the welfare of the *Sumsumâra* mountain, near *Bhugga*, he dwelt in the wilderness of *Bhesakala*. The ninth year at *Kosambi*. The tenth year in the *Pârileyyaka* wilderness. The eleventh year in the brâhman village *Nâlâ*. The twelfth at *Verañja*. The thirteenth at the *Cali* mountain. The fourteenth at the *Jetavanamahâvihâra*, in *Sâvatthipura*. The fifteenth at the great city *Kapilavatthu*. The sixteenth at *Alavi*, subduing *Alavako* (an evil spirit); and administering the heavenly draught to eighty-four thousand living creatures. The seventeenth at *Râjagaha*. The eighteenth at the *Cali* mountain. The nineteenth at the same place, and he resided the twentieth at *Râjagaha*. From that period he exclusively dwelt either at the *Jetavanamahâvihâra* for the spiritual welfare of *Sâvatthipura* or at *Pubbârâma* for the welfare of *Sâketapura*, deriving his subsistence by alms (from those cities). On Satthâ (the divine teacher Sakya) becoming Buddha, he held his first *vassa* at the *Isipatana*, an edifice situated at *Bârânasi*, at a place

Migadâye paṭhamavassaṃ vasitvâ vutthavasso pavâretvâ Uruvelaṃ gantvâ tattha tayo mâse va santo te bhâtikajaṭile dametvâ bhikkhusahassena kataparivâro Phussamâsapuṇṇamâyaṃ Râjagahaṃ gantvâ dve mâse tatth' eva vasi: tadâ Bârâṇasito nikkhantassa pan' assa pañcamâsâ jâtâ sakalo hemanto atikkanto Udâyittherassa âgata-divasato sattaṭṭhadivasâ vinivattâ so Phaggunamâsiyaṃ cintesi:—atikkanto hemanto vasantakâlo anuppatto samayo Tathâgatassa Kapilapuraṃ gantun ti. So evaṃ cintetvâ kulanagaragamanatthâya saṭṭhimattâhi gâthâhi gamanavaṇṇaṃ vaṇṇeti.

Atha satthâ tassa vacanaṃ sutvâ ñâtisaṅgahaṃ kâtukâmo Aṅgamagadhavâsînaṃ kulaputtânaṃ dasahi sahassehi Kapilavatthuvâsînaṃ dasahi sahassehî ti sabbe yeva vîsatiyâ khîṇâsavasahassehi parivuto Râjagahato nikkhamitvâ divase divase yojanaṃ gacchanto Râjagahato saṭṭhiyojanaṃ Kapilapuraṃ dvîhi mâsehi pâpuṇitvâ tattha ñâtinam vandâpanatthaṃ yamaka-pâṭihâriyaṃ akâsi tadâyaṃ Buddhavaṃso desito.

Kassa vacanan ti? Sâvakapaccekabuddhânaṃ asâdhâra-

---

so secluded that no wild animal was disturbed; and having completed his *vassa* there, repaired to *Uruvela*, where he tarried three months. Having there converted three *jaṭilas* (ascetics) who were brothers, attended by his fraternity of a thousand *bhikkhus*, he proceeded to *Râjagaha* on the full-moon day of the month Mâya (January—February), and there sojourned two months. Five months had then elapsed since his departure from *Bârânasi*. The *hemanta* was also over; and it was also seven or eight days after the arrival of the emissary *Udâyi*. That individual, in the month of *Phagguna* (February—March), thus thought, "The *hemanta* is past, and the *vasanta* (first half of the hot season) is arrived, and it is the time *Tathâgata* promised to repair to *Kapilavatthu*." Having thus reflected, he set forth the gratifications of a visit to his native city in a poem of sixty verses (to Buddha).

Thereupon *Satthâ*, on his hearing of this appeal, disposed to gratify the wishes of his relatives, attended by ten thousand *bhikkhus* of various tribes, from *Aṅga* and *Magadha*, and by ten thousand from *Kapilavatthu*, being altogether twenty thousand sanctified *arahats*, set out from *Râjagaha*. By only travelling daily at the rate of one *yojana*, he reached the city of *Kapilavatthu*, which is distant from *Râjagaha* sixty *yojanas*, in two months; and in order that he might command the reverence of his relations, he performed a miracle of two opposite results.

It was upon this occasion that he propounded the *Buddhavaṃsa*.

ṇaṃ sammâsambuddhass' eva vacanaṃ. Kena câbhato ti? Acâriyaparamparâya âgato ayaṃ hi Sâriputtatthero Bhaddaji Tissokosiyaputto Siggavo Moggaliputto Sudatto Dhammiko Dâsako Sonako Revato ti evam âdîhi yâva tatiyasaṅgîtikâlo âbhato. Tato uddham pi tesaṃ yeva sissânusissehî ti evaṃ tâva âcariyaparamparâya yâv' ajja kâlaṃ âbhato ti veditabbo. Ettâvatâ kenâyaṃ desito kattha kassatthâya ca desito kimatthâya kadâ kassa vacanaṃ kena câbhato ti. Ayaṃ kathâ [1] vuttatthâ hoti evaṃ âbhatassa pan' assa idâni atthavaṇṇanâ hoti.

Sâ panâyaṃ atthavaṇṇanâ yasmâ dûre nidânaṃ avidûre nidânaṃ santike nidânan ti imâni tîṇi nidânâni dassetvâ vaṇṇitâ suvaṇṇitâ nâma hoti. Ye ca naṃ suṇanti tehi samudâgamato paṭṭhâya viññâtattâ suviññâtâ va hoti tasmâ hi tâhi nidânâni dassetvâ va vannayissâma.

Tattha âdito tâva tesaṃ nidânânaṃ nâma paricchedo veditabbo.

Whose discourse is it? It is the discourse of the supreme *Buddha* who is not to be compared with the priesthood and the *Páccekabuddhas*.

By whom has it been perpetuated? It has been perpetuated by the generation or unbroken succession of the *theras* (elders of the priesthood). This is that succession:—SÂRIPUTTA thera, BHADDAJI, TISSOKOSIYAPUTTA, SIGGAVA, MOGGALIPUTTA, SUDATTA, DHAMMIKA, DASAKA, SONAKA, REVATA. By these it was brought to the period when the third convocation was held.

If it be asked, how has it subsequently (to the third convocation) been perpetuated by their disciples? Be it understood, that in the same manner, it has been brought down to the present day by the transmission from preceptor to disciple.

By thus much explanation alone it will be understood by whom, where, for whose edification, on whose account, and when it was propounded; whose discourse it was, and by whom it has been perpetuated. It now behoves unto the expounder of this commentary to enter upon his general explanation (of his work).

This *atthavaṇṇanâ* is the (*nidâna*) repository of the history in part of a remote antiquity; in part of comparatively modern, and in part of contemporaneous events. The illustration of these three portions of the history in a manner to be readily comprehended would be an important work. Those who attend thereto and acquire a knowledge thereof from the commencement would lay up

[1] MS. gâthâ.

Tatthâyaṃ saṅkhepato atthadîpanâ. Dîpaṅkaradasabalassa pâdamûle katâbhinîhârassa mahâsattassa yâva Vessantara-attabhâvâ cavitvâ Tusitabhavane nibbatti tâva pavattâ kathâ dûrenidânaṃ nâma: Tusitabhavanato cavitvâ yâva bodhimaṇḍe sabbaññutappatti tâva pavattâ kathâ avidûre nidânam nâma: santike nidânam pan' ekaṃ samayaṃ Bhagavâ Sâvatthiyaṃ viharati Jetavane Anâthapiṇḍikassa ârâme ti ca Râjagahe viharati Veluvane Kalandakanivâpe ti ca Vesâliyaṃ viharati Mahâvane kûṭâgârasâlâyan ti ca evaṃ mahâbodhimaṇḍe sabbaññutappattito yâva mahâparinibbânamañco etasmiṃ antare Bhagavâ yattha yattha vihâsi taṃ taṃ santike nidânaṃ nâmâ ti veditabbaṃ. Ettâvatâ saṅkhepen' eva tinnaṃ dûrâvidûrasantike nidânânaṃ vasena bâhira-nidâna-vaṇṇanâ samattâ hoti.

---

a store of valuable knowledge. I shall therefore enter upon the exposition of these *nidânas*, rendering their import manifest. Therein (in the study of this exposition) due notice should be taken of the division of the three *nidânas*. The nature (of the three *nidânas*) may be thus briefly explained:—the history extending from the age in which the sacred assurance was vouchsafed to the great being (*Mahâsatta*) at the feet of *Dîpaṅkara-buddha*, until by his death in the character of *Vessantara* he was reborn in the *Tusita-devaloka*, is called the *dûre-nidâna*, or the history of remote antiquity. The history extending from the translation by death from *Tusita* to the attainment of omniscience at the foot of the *bodhi* is called *avidûre-nidâna*, or comparatively modern history. The contemporaneous history contains records such as this, "At such a period Bhagava dwells at *Savatthi*, at the *Jetavanavihâra*, an edifice belonging to *Anâthapiṇḍika*, a dispenser of charity," "He dwells at *Râjagaha* at the *Veluvanavihâra* (the *vihâra* in a bamboo grove), at which the squirrels are regularly fed," "He dwells at *Vesâli* in the *Kûtâgâra* hall in the great wilderness." In this manner, whatever intervenes from the attainment of omniscience at the foot of the *bodhi* tree until his death-bed scene in obtaining the "great-decease," whatever takes place in the interval, be it understood that wherever he may have tarried, is included under the *santike nidâna*, resident or contemporaneous history. In these few words an explanation exclusively of the *nidâna*, *dûre*, *avidûre* and *santike* has been afforded.

THE CARIYÂ-PIṬAKA.

THE Cariyâ-Piṭaka, one of the fifteen books of the *Khuddaka-nikâya*, is a series of metrical tales of Gotama-Buddha in previous states of existence. They set forth briefly the lofty means (the *dasa pâramiyo*) by which he attained to the Buddhahood.

The thirty-five stories in this poetical compilation are all *Jâtaka*-tales, and are based upon similar narratives in the Pâli Jâtaka-book. In fact, these "birth-stories" presuppose a familiar acquaintance with all the incidents of the corresponding prose tales, so that the mere mention of the *Kapirâja* or *Sacca* birth would serve to recall to the mind of the hearer or reader all the chief incidents of the well-known Jâtaka-tale, much in the same way as the simple allusion to one of the New Testament parables (the Good Samaritan or the Prodigal Son) would be thoroughly understood without any further reference to the main points of the narrative. We are not therefore surprised to find that the metrical Jâtakas are much shorter than the prose tales (compare the *Kurudhamma-cariyaṁ* and its eight verses with the Jâtaka No. 276).

In the former version, moreover, the writer was chiefly concerned in bringing out the moral element, and he consequently leaves out of view the humour, fun, and even moral of the older stories (compare the *Mahiṃsarâjacariyaṃ* with Jâtaka No. 275).

One story (Book III. viii. p. 97), consisting only of a single verse, omits all details, so that we have only the bare statement that Buddha in a former birth, by his truth, preserved the world. This brevity makes it somewhat difficult to harmonize the two versions of these old birth-stories.

In the *Kapirâjacariyaṃ* (III. vii. p. 97) the incidents are so few that one is not enabled to state whether this story be the same as the amusing *Suṃsumâra-jataka* (?=Vânarajâtaka, No. 342), No. 208, or not.

Two stories, III. ix. p. 98 (Jât. No. 35) and III. x. p. 99 (Jât. No. 75) contain verses from the Jâtaka-book. The quotation in the Cariyâ-Piṭaka (line 11, p. 98) supplies a reading which sets right the faulty metre of the printed text (see Prof. Fausböll's Jâtaka, i. p. 215).

Ten of the stories in the present work may be compared with corresponding birth-tales in Dr. Fausböll's edition of the Jâtakas :—

Book	I.	3.	Kurudhamma-cariyaṃ	=	No.	276	of Jâtaka-book.
„	I.	4.	Mahâsudassana	„ =	„	95	„
„	I.	10.	Sasapaṇḍita	„ =	„	316	„
„	II.	1.	Sîlavanâga	„ =	„	72	„[1]
„	II.	5.	Mahiṃsa	„ =	„	275	„
„	III.	7.	Kapirâja	„ =	„	208	„
„	III.	9.	Vaṭṭapotaka	„ =	„	35	„
„	III.	10.	Maccharâja	„ =	„	75	„
„	III.	14.	Ekarâja	„ =	„	303	„
„	III.	15.	Mahâlomahaṃsa	„ =	„	94?	„

With the aid of Westergaard's *Codices Orientales Bibliothecæ Regiæ Harniensis* (pp. 36–42), we see that nearly all the other stories of the Cariyâ-Piṭaka, inaccessible as yet in print, have their originals in the Jâtaka-book, and may be here briefly given under the *Nipâta*, where they are found.

Saṇkha, Cûlabodhi, and Kaṇha-Dîpâyana belong to the *Dasanipâta*; Yudhañjaya to the *Ekâdasanipâta*; Akatti and Rururâja (=Rurumiga) are in the *Terasanipâta*; Sivi,[2] Campeyya, Mâtaṅga, Somanassa, Ayoghara, Bhisa, and Sacca

[1] See the *Mâtuposakajâtaka* (in the Ekadasanipâta of the Jâtaka-book), which may possibly resemble this story more than No. 72 does.

[2] For a Chinese version of this story, see Beal's *Buddhist Literature in China*, pp. 31-41.

form part of the *Vîsatinipata*; Jayaddisa belongs to the *Timsanipâta*; Saṅkhapâla to the *Cattâlîsanipâta*; Soṇa (=Soṇananda) to the *Sattatinipâta*; Nimirâja,[1] Vessantara,[2] Bhûridatta, Temiya (=Mûgapakkha), Sutasoma (=Mahâsutasoma?), and Suvaṇṇa-sâma (=Sâma) are in the last series, the *Asîtinipâta*.

I have failed, however, to trace the following three stories to their source:—1. *Mahâgovinda*. 2. *Dhammâdhamma* (=Mittâmittajâtaka in the *Dvâdasanipata*?). 3. *Candakumâra*.[3]

The Cariyâ-Piṭaka is divided into three parts. The first book treats of DÂNAPÂRAMITÂ,[4] and is illustrated by ten stories; the second has also ten stories in illustration of SÎLAPÂRAMITÂ; the third and last part deals with other sections of the *Dasa pâramiyo* as follows:—The first five stories refer to *pariccâga*, and serve to illustrate NEKKHAMMA-PÂRAMITÂ. The PÂRAMITÂS of *paññâ*, *viriyaṃ*, and *khanti* are entirely passed over unnoticed, though the writer could not fail to find some suitable stories with reference to these "perfections" in the Jâtaka-book.

ADHIṬṬHÂNA-PÂRAMITÂ has only one story devoted to it (No. VI.); SACCAPÂRAMITÂ is illustrated by six stories (Nos. VII.-XII.); METTÂPÂRAMITÂ by two (Nos. XIII. and XIV.); and UPEKHÂPÂRAMITÂ by one (No. XV.).

To a certain extent *paññâ*, *viriyaṃ*, *khanti*, *adhiṭṭhânaṃ*, and *upekhâ* are involved in the other pâramitas, and this perhaps may account for the omission of the first three, and the slight treatment of the last two perfections.[5]

The author of the Cariyâ-Piṭaka probably intended to devote an equal number of stories to each of the *Dasa-pâramiyo*; and had he done so, then we should have possessed ten books containing one hundred stories.

[1] Bigandet's *Legend of the Buddha*, vol. ii. pp. 162-166.

[2] See Hardy's *Manual of Buddhism*, 2nd ed. p. 101; Schiefner's *Tibetan Tales* (ed. Ralston), pp. 257-272.

[3] The Mâhagovinda, Dhammâdhamma and Candakumâra are alluded to in the Milindapañha, pp. 200-203.

[4] For a translation of these terms and some other particulars not repeated here, see Dr. Rhys Davids's *Buddhist Birth Stories* (pp. liii, liv) and Hardy's *Manual of Buddhism* (pp. 50, 100, 177, 342).

[5] For an English translation of the *Dânapâramitâ*, by the Rev. D. T. Gogerley, see *Journal of the Ceylon Branch of the Royal Asiatic Society*, 1853.

The JÂTAKA-MÂLÂ contains thirty-five birth-stories, ten of which have titles identical with the Cariyâ-Piṭaka tales.[1]

In the MAHÂVASTU we find the *Kapirâjacariyaṃ* under the title of "the story of the Porpoise" (=the *Suṃsumâra-jâtaka*), as well as the *Vânarajâtaka* and *Mahâgovindacariyaṃ*.

The BHADRAKALPA-AVADÂNA contains the stories of *Sîla-vanâga* and *Sutasoma*.

The BODHISATTVA-AVADÂNA relates the *Sivi, Sasa, Matsya, Vaṭṭapotaka, Ruru* and *Sutasoma* birth-stories.

It also has the *Buddhabodhijâtaka*, which resembles the Cûlabodhicariyaṃ of the Cariyâ-Piṭaka.[2]

As far as regards the grammatical peculiarities, there is not much to be said. Professor Fausböll has already pointed out, in his "Introduction to the *Sutta-Nipâta*" (pp. xii, xiii), the forms, grammatical and lexicographical, common to Pâli poetry. The Cariyâ-Piṭaka seems to have more of such peculiarities than the *Buddhavaṃsa*. The phrase *Kusale dasah' upâgato* (I. ii. l. 1, p. 74) Dr. Oldenberg has already noticed in Zeitschrift für vergl. Sprachf. N. F. v. 3, p. 320. He also refers to *Buddhavaṃsa*, II. l. 32, p. 8.[3]

We sometimes find the preposition more or less movable, as (in II. 4, l. 9, p. 86) vuḍḍhituṃ pari (=parivuḍḍhituṃ). More curious still are *ajjha so vasi* (p. 64, l. 5) and *ajjha 'haṃ vasiṃ* (p. 65, l. 14), in which the prefix and augment are separated from the verb. The form *kyâham* (l. 9, p. 87) =ke +aham, where *ke* has the force of *kiṃ* or *kena*, cf. *tayidam*= te-idaṃ, where *te*=*tad* or *taṃ*; *ye* for *yad* or *yam* is not uncommon. These may be locatives used adverbially, but see Dr. Trenckner's Pâli Miscellany, p. 75.

In this edition of the Cariyâ-Piṭaka, I have mainly followed the Additional MSS. 935, 936, in the University Library, Cambridge, written on paper in Siṅhalese characters. No. 935 contains the text, copied from a good MS. in the wihâra at

[1] See Dr. Davids's reference to a tradition respecting a similar work by Asvaghosha, *Buddhist Birth-stories*, p. liv.

[2] See "The Sanskrit Buddhist Literature of Nepal," by Râjendralâla Mitra, LL.D., C.I.E., pp. 44, 46, 50, 51, 52, 55, 56, 138, 146, 153. Calcutta, 1882.

[3] I venture to think that *kusale* is merely a contracted form for *kusalehi*, just as we find *tumhe* for *tumhehi* (Jât. i. p. 124).

Galle. No. 936 has no text, but presents all the variant readings of four manuscripts belonging to Degalla and Dadalla wiharas.[1]

Of these MSS. two (one from Dadalla, and the other from Degalla) are in Siṅhalese writing. The other two are Burmese MSS., and on these Dr. Rhys Davids has made the following note on a fly-leaf of the transcript, No. 936 :—

"The Burmese book and Burmese commentary are not by the same hand, but apparently of about equal age. They were brought to Dadalla wihare by Bopâgoda Unnanse, the Nâyaka Unnanse of the Amarâpura sect, who went to Burma about fifty years ago and there received Upasampadâ. He died about five years ago. His most distinguished pupil is Laṅkâgoda Unnanse, of Dewetagoda Wihara in Colombo.

"The other two books are each about thirty years old. (Galle, Nov. 3rd, 1869.)"

I have, also, carefully collated these with the Phayre MS. in the India Office Library. I have not had the advantage of any commentary, but expect shortly to have one from Ceylon. Part II. will contain various readings and extracts from the Commentary.

I here take the opportunity of acknowledging the kindness of Dr. Rost and Mr. Henry Bradshaw for the loan of valuable MSS. from their respective libraries. My best thanks are due to Dr. Frankfurter for collating my transcript of the Buddhavaṃsa with the Wilson MS. at Oxford, and to my friend Dr. Rhys Davids (who has drawn me away from my old love) for many valuable suggestions from time to time, and for the interest he has at all times taken in these humble efforts of mine to do something towards augmenting the number of Pâli Texts.

[1] These MSS. were copied for Dr. Rhys Davids by Dewa Aranolis, who evidently bestowed much pains and care upon his accurate transcripts.

TABLE OF CONTENTS.

BUDDHAVAṂSA.

Namo tassa bhagavato arahato sammâsambuddhassa.

I.

THE GEM-CAṄKAMA SECTION.

1 Brahmâ ca lokâdhipati sahampati katañjalî anadhivaraṃ ayâcatha :—
santîdha sattâ apparajakkhajâtikâ desehi dhammaṃ anukampî maṃ pajaṃ.
2 Sampannavijjâcaraṇassa tâdino jutîndharass' antimadehadhârino
Tathâgatass' appaṭipuggalassa uppajji kâruññatâ sabbasatte.
3 Na bho te jânanti sadevamânusâ Buddho ayaṃ kîdisako naruttamo
iddhibalaṃ paññâbalañ ca kîdisaṃ Buddhabalaṃ lokahitassa kîdisaṃ.
4 Na bho te jânanti sadevamânusâ buddho ayaṃ edisako naruttamo
iddhibalaṃ paññâbalañ ca edisaṃ Buddhabalaṃ lokahitassa edisaṃ.
5 Handâhaṃ dassayissâmi Buddhabalaṃ anuttaraṃ
caṅkamaṃ mâpayissâmi nabhe ratanamaṇḍitaṃ.
6 Bhummâ mahârâjikâ tâvatiṃsâ yâmâ ca devâ tusitâ ca nimmitâ
paranimmitâ ye pi ca brahmakâyikâ ânanditâ vipulaṃ akaṃsu ghosaṃ.

7 Obhâsitâ ca paṭhavî sadevakâ puthû ca lokantarikâ asamvutâ
tamo ca tibbo vihato tadâ ahu disvâna accherakaṃ pâṭihîraṃ.
8 Sadevagandhabbamanussarakkhase âbhâ ulârâ vipulâ ajâyatha
imasmiṃ loke parasmiṃ cobhayasmiṃ adho ca uddhaṃ tiriyañ ca vitthataṃ.
9 Sattuttamo anadhivaro vinâyako satthâ ahu devamanussapûjito
mahânubhâvo satapuññalakkhaṇo dassesi accherakaṃ pâṭihîraṃ.
10 So yâcito devavarena cakkhumâ atthaṃ samekkhitvâ tadâ naruttamo
caṅkamaṃ tattha mâpayi lokanâyiko suniṭṭhitaṃ sabbaratananimmitaṃ.
11 Iddhî ca âdesanânusâsanî tipâṭihîre Bhagavâ vasî ahu
caṅkamanaṃ mâpayi lokanâyako suniṭṭhittaṃ sabbaratananimmitaṃ.
12 Dasasahassi-lokadhâtuyâ Sinerupabbatuttame
thambhe va dassesi paṭipâṭiyâ caṅkame ratanâmaye.
13 Dasasahassî atikkamma caṅkamaṃ mâpayi Jino
sabbasovaṇṇayâ passe caṅkame ratanâmaye.
14 Tûlâ saṅghâṭânuvaggâ sovaṇṇaphalakatthatâ
vedikâ sabbasovaṇṇâ-d-ubhato passe sunimmitâ
15 Maṇimuttavâlukâ kiṇṇâ nimmitâ ratanâmayâ
obhâseti disâ sabbâ sataraṃsî va uggato.
16 Tasmiṃ caṅkamane dhîro dvattiṃsavaralakkhaṇo
virocamâno sambuddho caṅkame caṅkami Jino.
17 Dibbaṃ mandâravaṃ pupphaṃ padumaṃ pâricchattakaṃ
caṅkamane okiranti sabbe devâ samâgatâ.
18 Passanti taṃ devasaṅghâ dasasahassî pamoditâ
namassamânâ nipatanti tuṭṭhahaṭṭhâ pamoditâ.
19 Tâvatiṃsâ ca yâmâ ca tusitâ ca pi devatâ
nimmânaratino devâ ye devâ vasavattino
udaggacittâ sumanâ passanti lokanâyakaṃ.
20 Sadevagandhabbamanussarakkhasâ nâgâ supaṇṇâ atha vâpi kiṇṇarâ

passanti taṃ lokahitânukampakaṃ nabhe va accuggataṃ candamaṇḍalaṃ.
21 Âbhassarâ subhakiṇhâ vehapphalâ akaniṭṭhâ ca devatâ
susuddhasukkavatthavasanâ tiṭṭhanti pañjalîkatâ.
22 Muñcanti pupphaṃ pana pañcavaṇṇikaṃ mandâvaram candanacuṇṇamissitaṃ
bhamanti celâni ca ambare tadâ. aho Jino lokahitânukampako!
23 Tuvaṃ satthâ ca ketû ca dhajo yûpo ca pâṇinaṃ
parâyano patiṭṭho ca dvipo ca dvipaduttamo.
24 Dasasahassi-lokadhâtuyâ devatâyo mahiddhikâ
parivâretvâ namassanti tuṭṭhahaṭṭhâ pamoditâ.
25 Devatâ devakaññâ ca pasannâ tuṭṭhamânasâ
pañcavaṇṇikapupphehi pûjayanti narâsabhaṃ.
26 Passanti taṃ devasaṅghâ pasannâ tuṭṭhamânasâ
pañcavaṇṇikapupphehi pûjayanti narâsabhaṃ.
27 Aho acchariyaṃ loke abbhutaṃ lomahaṃsanaṃ!
nam' edisaṃ bhûtapubbaṃ accheraṃ lomahaṃsanaṃ!
28 Sakaṃ sakamhi bhavane nisîditvâna devatâ
hasanti mahâhasitaṃ disvân' accherakaṃ nabhe.
29 Âkâsaṭṭhâ ca bhummaṭṭhâ tiṇapanthanivâsino
katañjalî namassanti tuṭṭhahaṭṭhâ pamoditâ.
30 Ye pi dîghâyukâ nâgâ puññavanto mahiddhikâ
pamoditâ namassanti pûjayanti naruttamaṃ.
31 Saṅgîtiyo pavattanti ambare anilañjase
cammanaddhâni vâdenti disvân' accherakaṃ nabhe.
32 Saṅkhâ ca paṇavâ c' eva atho pi dindimâ bahû
antalikkhasmiṃ vajjanti disvân' accherakaṃ nabhe.
33 Abbhuto vata no ajja uppajji lomahaṃsano
dhuvam atthasiddhiṃ labbhâma khaṇo no paṭipâdito.
34 Buddho ti tesaṃ sutvâna pîti uppajji tâvade
Buddho Buddho ti kathayantâ tiṭṭhanti pañjalîkatâ.
35 Bhiṅkâraṃ sâdhukârañ ca ukkuṭṭhisampasâdanaṃ
pajâ vividhâ gagane vattanti pañjalîkatâ.
36 Gâyanti selenti ca vâdayanti ca bhujâni poṭhenti ca naccayanti ca
muñcanti pupphaṃ pana pañcavaṇṇikaṃ mandâravaṃ candanacuṇṇamissitaṃ.

37 Yathâ tuyhaṃ mahâvîra pâdesu cakkalakkhaṇaṃ
dhajavajirapaṭâkaṃ vaḍḍhamânaṅkusâvitaṃ.
38 Rûpe sîle samâdhimhi paññâya ca asâdiso
vimuttiyâ asamasamo dhammacakkappavattane.
39 Dasanâgabalaṃ kâye tuyhaṃ pâkatikaṃ balaṃ
iddhibalena asamo dhammacakkappavattane.
40 Evaṃ sabbaguṇûpetaṃ sabbaṅgasamupâgatam
mahâmuniṃ kâruṇikaṃ lokanâthaṃ namassatha!
41 Abhivâdanaṃ thomanaṃ vandanañ ca pasaṃsanaṃ
namassanañ ca pûjañ ca sabbaṃ arahasî tuvaṃ!
42 Ye keci loke vandaneyyâ vandanaṃ arahanti ye
sabbaseṭṭho mahâvîra sadiso te na vijjati!
43 Sâriputto mahâpañño samâdhijhânakovido
Gijjhakûṭe ṭhito yeva passati lokanâyakaṃ.
44 Suphullaṃ sâlarâjam va candaṃ va gagane yathâ
majjhantike va suriyaṃ oloketi narâsabhaṃ.
45 Jalantaṃ dîparukkhaṃ va taruṇasuriyaṃ va uggataṃ
byâmappabhânurañjitaṃ dhîraṃ passati nâyakaṃ.
46 Pañcannaṃ bhikkhusatânaṃ katakiccânaṃ tâdinaṃ
khîṇâsavânaṃ vimalânaṃ khaṇena sannipâtayi.
47 Lokappasâdanaṃ nâma pâṭihîraṃ nidassayi
amhe pi tattha gantvâna vandissâma mayaṃ Jinaṃ.
48 Etha sabbe gamissâma pucchissâma mayaṃ Jinaṃ
kaṅkhaṃ vinodayissâma passitvâ lokanâyakaṃ.
49 Sâdhû ti te paṭisutvâ nipakâ saṃvutindriyâ
pattacîvaraṃ âdâya taramânâ upâgamuṃ.
50 Khîṇâsavehi vimalehi dantehi uttame dame
Sâriputto mahâpañño iddhiyâ upasaṅkami.
51 Tehi bhikkhûhi parivuto Sâriputto mahâgaṇî
laḷanto devo gagane iddhiyâ upasaṅkami.
52 Ukkâsitañ ca khipitaṃ ajjhupekkhitvâ subbatâ
sagâravâ sappaṭissâ sambuddhaṃ upasaṅkamuṃ.
53 Upasaṅkamitvâ passanti sayambhuṃ lokanâyakaṃ
nabhe accugataṃ dhîraṃ candaṃ va gagane yathâ.
54 Jalantaṃ dîparukkhaṃ va vijjû va gagane yathâ
majjhantike va suriyaṃ passanti lokanâyakaṃ.
55 Pañcabhikkhusatâ sabbe passanti lokanâyakaṃ
rahadam iva vippasannaṃ suphullaṃ padumaṃ yathâ.

56 Añjaliṃ paggahetvâna tuṭṭhahaṭṭhâ pamoditâ
namassamânâ nipatanti satthuno cakkalakkhaṇe.
57 Sâriputto mahâpañño Koraṇḍasamasâdiso
samâdhijhânakusalo vandati lokanâyakaṃ.
58 Gajjito kâlamegho va nîluppalasamasâdiso
iddhibalena asamo Moggalâno mahiddhiko.
59 Mahâkassapo pi ca thero utattakanakasannibho
dhûtaguṇe agganikhitto thomito satthuvaṇṇito.
60 Dibbacakkhûnaṃ yo aggo Anuruddho mahâgaṇî
ñâtiseṭṭho Bhagavato avidûre va tiṭṭhati.
61 Âpatti-anâpattiyâ satikiccâya kovido .
vinaye agganikkhitto Upâli satthuvaṇṇito.
62 Sukhumanipuṇatthapaṭividdho kathikânam pavaro gaṇî
Isimantâniyâ putto Puṇṇo nâmâ ti vissuto.
63 Etesaṃ cittam aññâya opammakusalo muni
khaṅkhacchedo mahâvîro kathesi attano guṇaṃ.
64 Cattâro te asaṅkheyyâ koṭi yesaṃ na ñâyati
sattakâyo ca âkâso cakkavâḷâ ca anantakâ
Buddhañâṇaṃ appameyyaṃ na sakkâ ete vijânituṃ.
65 Kiṃ etaṃ acchariyaṃ loke yam me iddhi-vikubbanaṃ
aññe bahû acchariyâ abbhutâ lomahaṃsaṇâ.
66 Yadâhaṃ tusite kâye santusito nâm' ahaṃ tadâ
dasasahassî samâgamma yâcanti p' añjalî mamaṃ.
67 Kâlo deva mahâvîra uppajja mâtu kucchiyaṃ
sadevakan târayanto bujjhassu amataṃ padaṃ.
68 Tusitâ kâyâ cavitvâna yadâ okkami kucchiyaṃ
dasasahassî lokadhâtu kampittha dharaṇî tadâ.
69 Yadâhaṃ mâtu kucchito sampajâno va nikkhamiṃ
sâdhukâraṃ pavattenti dasasahassî pakampatha.
70 Okkanti me samo n' atthi jâtito abhinikkhame
sambodhiyaṃ ahaṃ seṭṭho dhammacakkappavattane.
71 Aho acchariyaṃ loke buddhânam guṇamahantatâ
dasasahassî lokadhâtu chabbikâraṃ pakampatha !
72 Obhâso ca mahâ âsi accheraṃ lomahaṃsanaṃ
Bhagavâ ca tamhi samaye lokajeṭṭho narâsabho.
73 Sadevakaṃ dassayanto iddhiyâ caṅkami Jino
caṅkame caṅkamanto va kathesi lokanâyako
antarâ na nivatteti catuhatthe caṅkame yathâ.

74 Sâriputto mahâpañño samâdhijhânakovido
paññâya pâramippatto pucchati lokanâyakaṃ :—
75 Kîdiso te mahâvîra abhinîhâro naruttama
kamhi kâle tayâ dhîra patthitâ bodhimuttamâ?
76 Dânaṃ sîlañ ca nekkhammaṃ paññâ-viriyañ ca kîdisaṃ
khanti-saccaṃ adhiṭṭhânaṃ mettupekkhâ ca kîdisâ?
77 Dasapâramî tayâ dhîra kîdisa lokanâyaka
kathaṃ upapâramî puṇṇâ paramatthapâramî kathaṃ?
78 Tassa puṭṭho vyâkâsi karavîkamadhuraṅgiro
nibbâpayanto hadayaṃ hâsayanto sadevakaṃ.
79 Atîtabuddhânaṃ jinânaṃ desitaṃ nikîḷitam buddhaparamparâgataṃ
pubbe nivâsânugatâya buddhiyâ pakâsayî lokahitaṃ sadevake.
80 Pîtipâmojjajananaṃ sokasallavinodanaṃ
sabbasampatti-paṭilâbhaṃ cittikatvâ suṇotha me.
81 Madanimmadanaṃ sokanudaṃ saṃsâraparimocanaṃ
sabbadukkhakkhayaṃ maggaṃ sakkaccaṃ paṭipajjathâ ti.

RATANACAṄKAMANAKAṆḌAṂ NIṬṬHITAṂ.

II.

DÎPAṄKARA THE FIRST BUDDHA.

1 Kappe ca satasahasse ca caturo ca asaṅkhiye
Amaram nâma nagaraṃ dassaneyyaṃ manoramaṃ
2 Dasahi saddehi avivittam annapânasamâyutaṃ.
hatthisaddaṃ assasaddaṃ bherisaṅkharathâni ca
3 Khâdatha pivatha c'eva annapânena ghositaṃ.
Nagaraṃ sabbaṅgasampannaṃ sabbakammam upâgataṃ.
4 Sattaratanasampannaṃ nânâjanasamâkulaṃ
samiddhaṃ devanagaraṃ âvâsaṃ puññakamminaṃ.
5 Nagare Amaravatiyâ Sumedho nâma brâhmaṇo
anekakoṭisannicayo pahûtadhanadhaññavâ.

6 Ajjhâyako mantadharo tiṇṇaṃ vedânapâragû
lakkhaṇe itihâse ca saddhamme pâramiṅgato.
7 Rahogato nisîditvâ evaṃ cintes' ahaṃ tada :—
dukkho punabhavo nâma sarîrassa ca bhedanaṃ.
8 Jâtidhammo jarâdhammo vyâdhidhammo c'ahan tadâ
ajaraṃ amaraṃ khemaṃ pariyesissâmi nibbutiṃ.
9 Yan nûn imaṃ pûtikâyaṃ nânâkuṇapapûritaṃ
chaḍḍayitvâna gaccheyyaṃ anapekkho anatthiko.
10 Atthi hehî ti so maggo na so sakkâ na hetuye
pariyesissâmi taṃ maggaṃ bhavato parimuttiyâ ti.
11 Yathâpi dukkhe vijjante sukhaṃ nâma pi vijjati
evaṃ bhave vijjamâne vibhavo p'icchitabbako.
12 Yathâpi uṇhe vijjante aparaṃ vijjati sîtalaṃ
evaṃ tividhaggi vijjante nibbânaṃ icchitabbakaṃ.
13 Yathâ pi pâpe vijjante kalyâṇam api vijjati
evam eva jâti vijjante ajâtim p'icchitabbakaṃ.
14 Yathâ gûthagato puriso taḷâkaṃ disvâna pûritaṃ
na gavesati taṃ taḷâkuṃ na doso taḷâkassa so.
15 Evaṃ kilesamaladhove vijjante amatantale
na gavesati taṃ taḷâkaṃ na doso amatantale.
16 Yathâ arîhi pariruddho vijjante gamane pathe
na palâyati so puriso na doso añjasassa so.
17 Evaṃ kilesapariruddho vijjamâne sive pathe
na gavesati taṃ maggaṃ na doso sivamañjase.
18 Yathâpi vyâdhito puriso vijjamâne tikicchake
na tikicchâpeti taṃ vyâdhiṃ na doso tikicchake
19 Evaṃ kilesavyâdhîhi dukkhito paṭipîḷito
na gavesati taṃ âcariyaṃ na doso so vinâyake.
20 Yathâpi kuṇapaṃ puriso kaṇṭhe baddhaṃ jigucchiyaṃ
mocayitvâna gaccheyya sukhî serî sayaṃvasî.
21 Tath' ev' imaṃ pûtikâyaṃ nânâkuṇapasañcayaṃ
chaḍḍayitvâna gaccheyyaṃ anapekkho anatthiko.
22 Yathâ uccâraṭṭhânamhi karîsam naranâriyo
chaḍḍayitvâna gacchanti anapekkhâ anatthikâ
23 Evam evâhaṃ imaṃ kâyaṃ nânâkuṇapapûritaṃ
chaḍḍayitvâna gacchissaṃ vaccaṃ katvâ yathâ kuṭiṃ.
24 Yâthâpi jajjaraṃ nâvaṃ paluggaṃ udakagâhiniṃ
sâmî chaḍḍetvâ gacchanti anapekkhâ anatthikâ

25 Evam evâhaṃ imaṃ kâyaṃ navacchiddaṃ dhuvassavaṃ
chaḍḍayitvâna gacchissam jiṇṇanâvaṃ va sâmikâ.
26 Yathâpi puriso corehi gacchanto bhaṇḍaṃ âdiya.
bhaṇḍacchedabhayaṃ disvâ chaḍḍayitvâna gacchati
27 Evam eva ayaṃ kâyo mahâcorasamo viya
pahây' imaṃ gamissâmi kusalacchedanâbhayâ ti.
28 Evâhaṃ cintayitvâna nekakoṭisatam dhanaṃ
Nâthânâthânaṃ datvâna Himavantaṃ upâgamiṃ.
29 Himavantass' avidûre Dhammako nâma pabbato
assamo sukato mayhaṃ paṇṇasâlâ sumâpitâ.
30 Caṅkamaṃ tattha mâpesiṃ pañcadosa-vivajjitaṃ
aṭṭhaguṇasamûpetaṃ abhiññâbalaṃ âhariṃ.
31 Sâṭakaṃ pajahiṃ tattha navadosasamupâgataṃ
vâkacîraṃ nivâsesiṃ dvâdasaguṇupâgataṃ.
32 Aṭṭhadosasamâkiṇṇaṃ pajahiṃ paṇṇasâlakaṃ
upâgamiṃ rukkhamûlaṃ guṇe dasah' upâgataṃ.
33 Vâpitaṃ ropitaṃ dhaññaṃ pajahiṃ niravasesato
anekaguṇasampannaṃ pavattaphalam âdiyim.
34 Tattha padhânaṃ padahiṃ nisajjaṭṭhânacaṅkame
abbhantaramhi sattâhe abhiññâbalam pâpuṇin ti.
35 Evam me siddhippattassa vasîbhûtassa sâsane
Dîpaṅkaro nâma jino uppajji lokanâyako.
36 Uppajjante ca jâyante bujjhante dhammadesane
caturo nimitte nâddasiṃ jhânaratisamappito.
37 Paccantadesavisaye nimantetvâ Tathâgataṃ
tassa âgamanaṃ maggaṃ sodhenti tuṭṭhamânasâ.
38 Ahan tena samayena nikkhamitvâ sakassamâ
dhunanto vâkacîrâni gacchâmi ambare tadâ.
39 Vedajâtaṃ janaṃ disvâ tuṭṭhahaṭṭhaṃ pamoditaṃ
orohitvâna gaganâ mânuse pucchi tâvade.
40 Tuṭṭhahaṭṭho pamodito vedajâto mahâjano
kassa sodhîyati maggo añjasaṃ vaṭumâyanan ti?
41 Te me puṭṭhâ vyâkaṃsu buddho loke anuttaro
Dîpaṅkaro nâma jino uppajji lokanâyako
tassa sodhîyati maggo añjasaṃ vaṭumâyanaṃ.
42 Buddho ti mama sutvâna pîti uppâjji tâvade
Buddho buddho ti kathayanto somanassaṃ pavedayim.
43 Tattha ṭhatvâ vicintesiṃ tuṭṭho saṃviggamânaso :

Idha bîjâni ropissaṃ khaṇe ve mâ upaccagâ.
44 Yadi buddhassa sodhetha ekokâsam dadâtha me
Ahaṃ pi sodhayissâmi añjasaṃ vaṭumâyanaṃ.
45 Adaṃsu te mam okâsaṃ sodhetuṃ añjasaṃ tadâ
Buddho buddho ti cintento maggaṃ sodhem' ahaṃ tadâ.
46 Aniṭṭhite mam okâse Dîpaṅkaro mahâmuni
cattûhi satasahassehi chalabhiññehi tâdihi
khîṇâsavehi vimalehi paṭipajji añjasaṃ jino.
47 Paccuggamanâ vattanti vajjanti bheriyo bahû
âmoditâ naramarû sâdhukâraṃ pavattayuṃ.
48 Devamanusse passanti manussâ pi ca devatâ
ubho pi te pañjalikâ anuyanti Tathâgataṃ.
49 Devâ dibbehi turiyehi manussâ mânusakehi ca
ubho pi te vajjayantâ anuyanti Tathâgataṃ.
50 Dibbaṃ mandâravaṃ pupphaṃ padumaṃ pâricchattakaṃ
disodisaṃ okiranti âkâsa-nabhagatâ marû.
51 Campakaṃ saḷalaṃ nîpaṃ nâgapunnâgaketakaṃ
disodisaṃ ukkhipanti bhûmitalagatâ narâ.
52 Kese muñcitvâhaṃ tattha vâkacîrañ ca cammakaṃ
kalale pattharitvâna avakujjo nipajj' ahaṃ.
53 Akkamitvâna maṃ buddho saha sissehi gacchatu
mâ naṃ kalale akkamittho hitâya me bhavissatî ti.
54 Paṭhaviyaṃ nipannassa evam me âsi cetaso
icchamâno ahaṃ ajja kilese jhâpaye mamaṃ.
55 Kim me aññâtavesena dhammaṃ sacchikaten' idha
sabbaññutaṃ pâpuṇitvâ buddho hessaṃ sadevake.
56 Kim me ekena tiṇṇena purisena thâmadassinâ
sabbaññutaṃ pâpuṇitvâ santâressaṃ sadevake.
57 Iminâ me adhikârena katena purisuttame
sabbaññutaṃ pâpuṇâmi târemi janataṃ bahuṃ.
58 Saṃsârasotaṃ chinditvâ viddhaṃsetvâ tayo bhave
dhammanâvaṃ samâruyha santâressaṃ sadevake.
59 Manussattaṃ liṅgasampattihetu satthâra-dassanaṃ
pabbajâ guṇasampatti adhikâro ca chandatâ
aṭṭhadhammasamodhânâ abhinîhâro samijjhati.
60 Dîpaṅkaro lokavidû âhutînaṃ paṭiggaho
ussîsake maṃ ṭhatvâna idaṃ vacanam abravi:—
61 Passatha imaṃ tâpasaṃ jaṭilaṃ uggatâpanaṃ

aparimeyye ito kappe buddho loke bhavissati.
62 Atha Kapilavhayâ rammâ nikkhamitvâ Tathâgato
Padhânaṃ padahitvâna katvâ dukkarakâriyaṃ.
63 Ajapâlarukkhamûlasmiṃ nisîditvâ Tathâgato
tattha pâyâsam aggayha Nerañjaraṃ upehiti.
64 Nerañjarâya tîramhi pâyâsaṃ âdâ so jino
paṭiyattavaramaggena bodhimûlamhi ehiti.
65 Tato padakkhiṇaṃ katvâ bodhimaṇḍaṃ anuttaro
assattharukkhamûlamhi bujjhissati mahâyaso.
66 Imassa janikâ mâtâ Mâyâ nâma bhavissati
pitâ Suddhodano nâma ayaṃ hessati Gotamo.
67 Anâsavâ vîtamalâ santacittâ samâhitâ
Kolito Upatisso ca aggâ hessanti sâvakâ.
68 Ânando nâm' upaṭṭhâko upaṭṭhissati taṃ jinaṃ
Khemâ Uppalavaṇṇâ ca aggâ hessanti sâvikâ.
69 Anâsavâ vîtamalâ santacittâ samâhitâ
bodhi tassa bhagavato Assattho ti pavuccati.
70 Citto ca Hatthâḷavako aggâ hessant' upaṭṭhakâ
Nandamâtâ ca Uttarâ aggâ hessant' upaṭṭhikâ.
71 Idaṃ sutvâna vacanaṃ asamassa mahesino
âmoditâ naramarû : buddhabîjaṅkuro ayaṃ.
72 Ukkuṭṭhisaddâ vattanti appoṭhenti hasanti ca
katañjalî namassanti dasasahassî sadevakâ.
73 Yad' imassa lokanâthassa virajjhissâma sâsanaṃ
anâgatamhi addhâne hessâma sammukhâ imaṃ.
74 Yathâ manussâ nadiṃ tarantâ paṭititthaṃ virajjhiya
heṭṭhâtitthe gahetvâna uttaranti mahânadiṃ
75 Evaṃ evaṃ mayaṃ sabbe yadi muñcâm' imaṃ jinaṃ
anâgatamhi addhâne hessâma sammukhâ imaṃ.
76 Dîpaṅkaro lokavidû âhutînaṃ paṭiggaho
mama kammaṃ pakittetvâ dakkhiṇaṃ padaṃ uddhari.
77 Ye tatthâsuṃ jinaputtâ sabbe padakkhiṇaṃ akaṃsu maṃ
devâ manussâ asurâ ca abhivâdetvâna pakkamuṃ.
78 Dassanaṃ me atikkante sasaṅghe lokanâyake
sayanâ vuṭṭhahitvâna pallaṅkaṃ âbhujiṃ tadâ.
79 Sukhena sukhito homi pâmujjena pamodito
pîtiyâ ca abhissanno pallaṅkaṃ âbhujiṃ tadâ.
80 Pallaṅkena nisîditvâ evaṃ cintes' ahaṃ tadâ :

vasîbhûto ahaṃ jhâne abhiññâsu pâramiṅgato
81 Sahassiyambhi lokambhi isayo n' atthi me samâ
asamo iddhidhammesu alabhiṃ îdisaṃ sukhaṃ.
82 Pallaṅkâbhujane mayhaṃ dasasahassâdhivâsino
mahânâdaṃ pavattesuṃ dhuvaṃ buddho bhavissasi.
83 Yâ pubbe bodhisattânaṃ pallaṅkavaram âbhuje
nimittâni padissanti tâni ajja padissare.
84 Sîtaṃ vyapagataṃ hoti uṇhañ ca upasammati
tâni ajja padissanti dhuvaṃ buddho bhavissasi.
85 Dasasahassî lokadhâtu nissaddâ hoti nirâkulâ
tâni ajja padissanti dhuvam buddho bhavissasi.
86 Mahâvâtâ na vâyanti na sandanti savantiyo
tâni ajja padissanti dhuvaṃ buddho bhavissasi.
87 Thalajâ dakajâ pupphâ sabbe pupphanti tâvade
te p' ajja pupphitâ sabbe dhuvaṃ buddho bhavissasi.
88 Latâ vâ yadivâ rukkhâ phaladharâ honti tâvade
te p' ajja phalitâ sabbe dhuvaṃ buddho bhavissasi.
89 Âkâsaṭṭhâ ca bhummaṭṭhâ ratanâ jotanti tâvade
te p' ajja ratanâ jotanti dhuvaṃ buddho bhavissasi.
90 Mânusakâ ca dibbâ ca turiyâ vajjanti tâvade
te p' ajj ubho abhiravanti dhuvaṃ buddho bhavissasi.
91 Vicittapupphâ gaganâ abhivassanti tâvade
te pi ajja padissanti dhuvaṃ buddho bhavissasi.
92 Mahâsamuddo âbhujati dasasahassî pakampati
te pi ajj' ubho abhiravanti dhuvam buddho bhavissasi.
93 Niraye pi dasasahassî aggî nibbanti tâvade
te p' ajja nibbutâ aggî dhuvaṃ buddho bhavissasi.
94 Vimalo hoti suriyo sabbâ dissanti târakâ
te pi ajja padissanti dhuvaṃ buddho bhavissasi.
95 Anovaṭṭena udakaṃ mahîyâ ubbhijji tâvade
taṃ p' ajj' ubbhijjate mahîyâ dhuvaṃ bhavissasi.
96 Târâgaṇâ virocanti nakkhattâ gaganamaṇḍale
visâkhâ candimâyuttâ dhuvaṃ buddho bhavissasi.
97 Bilâsayâ darîsayâ nikkhamanti sakâsayâ
te p' ajja âsayâ chuddhâ dhuvaṃ buddho bhavissasi.
98 Na hoti arati sattânaṃ santuṭṭhâ honti tâvade
te p' ajja sabbe santuṭṭhâ dhuvaṃ buddho bhavissasi.
99 Rogâ tad' upasammanti jighacchâ ca vinassati

tâni ajja padissanti dhuvaṃ buddho bhavissasi.
100 Râgo tadâ tanu hoti doso moho vinassati
te p' ajja vigatâ sabbe dhuvaṃ buddho bhavissasi.
101 Bhayam tadâ na bhavati ajja p' etaṃ padissati
tena liṅgena jânâma dhuvaṃ buddho bhavissasi.
102 Rajo n' uddhaṃsati uddhaṃ ajja p' etaṃ padissati
tena liṅgena jânâma dhuvaṃ buddho bhavissasi.
103 Aniṭṭhagandho pakkamati dibbagandho pavâyati
so p' ajja vâyati gandho dhuvaṃ buddho bhavissasi.
104 Sabbe devâ padissanti ṭhapayitvâ arûpino
te p' ajja sabbe dissanti dhuvaṃ buddho bhavissasi.
105 Yâvatâ nirayâ nâma sabbe dissanti tâvade
te p' ajja sabbe dissanti dhuvaṃ buddho bhavissasi.
106 Kuḍḍâ kavâṭâ selâ ca na hontâvaraṇaṃ tadâ
âkâsabhûtâ te p'ajja dhuvaṃ buddho bhavissasi.
107 Cutî ca upapattî ca khaṇe tasmiṃ na vijjati
tâni p'ajja padissanti dhuvaṃ buddho bhavissasi.
108 Daḷhaṃ paggaṇha viriyaṃ mâ nivatta abhikkama
mayaṃ p'etaṃ vijânâma dhuvaṃ buddho bhavissasi.
109 Buddhassa vacanaṃ sutvâ dasasahassî na cubhayaṃ
tuṭṭhahaṭṭho pamodito evaṃ cintes' ahaṃ tadâ.
110 Advejjhavacanâ buddhâ amoghavacanâ jinâ
vitathaṃ n'atthi buddhânaṃ dhuvaṃ buddho bhavâm' ahaṃ.
111 Yathâ khittaṃ nabhe leḍḍu dhuvaṃ patati bhûmiyaṃ
tath' eva buddhaseṭṭhânaṃ vacanaṃ dhuvasassataṃ
vitathaṃ n' atthi buddhânaṃ dhuvaṃ buddho bhavâm' ahaṃ.
112 Yathâpi sabbasattânaṃ maraṇaṃ dhuvasassataṃ
tath' eva buddhaseṭṭhânaṃ vacanaṃ dhuvasassataṃ
vitathaṃ . . . pe . . . .
113 Yathâ rattikkhaye patte suriyass' uggamanaṃ dhuvaṃ
tath' eva buddhaseṭṭhânaṃ vacanaṃ dhuvasassataṃ
vitathaṃ . . . pe . . . .
114 Yathâ ṇikkhantasayanassa sîhassa nadanaṃ dhuvaṃ
tath' eva buddhaseṭṭhânaṃ vacanaṃ dhuvasassataṃ
vitathaṃ . . . pe . . . .
115 Yathâ âpannasattânaṃ bhâramoropanaṃ dhuvaṃ

tath' eva . . . pe . . . .
vitatham . . . pe . . . .
116 Handa buddhakare dhamme vicinâmi ito c' ito
uddhaṃ adho dasadisâ yâvatâ dhammadhâtuyâ.
117 Vicinanto tadâ dakkhiṃ paṭhamaṃ dânapâramiṃ
pubbakehi mahesîhi anuciṇṇaṃ mahâpathaṃ.
118 Imaṃ tvaṃ paṭhamaṃ tâva daḷhaṃkatvâ samâdiya
dânapâramitaṃ gaccha yadi bodhiṃ pattum icchasi
119 Yathâpi kumbho sampuṇṇo yassa kassaci adhokato
vamate vudakaṃ nissesaṃ na tattha parirakkhati
120 Tath'eva yâcake disvâ hînamukkaṭṭhaṃajjhime
dadâhi dânaṃ nissesaṃ kumbho viya adhokato.
121 Na h' ete ettakâ yeva buddhadhammâ bhavissare
aññe pi vicinissâmi ye dhammâ bodhipâcanâ
122 Vicinanto tadâ dakkhiṃ dutiyaṃ sîlapâramiṃ
pubbakehi mahesîhi âsevitanisevitaṃ.
123 Imaṃ tvaṃ dutiyaṃ tâva daḷhaṃkatvâ samâdiya
sîlapâramitaṃ gaccha yadi bodhiṃ pattum icchasi.
124 Yathâpi camarî vâḷaṃ kismici paṭivilaggitaṃ·
upeti maraṇaṃ tattha na vikopeti vâḷadhiṃ.
125 Tath' eva catûsu bhûmîsu sîlâni paripûriya
Parirakkha sabbadâ sîlaṃ camarî viya vâḷadhiṃ.
126 Na h' ete ettakâ yeva buddhadhammâ bhavissare
aññe pi vicinissâmi ye dhammâ bodhipâcanâ.
127 Vicinanto tadâ dakkhiṃ tatiyaṃ nekkhammapâramiṃ
pubbakehi mahesîhi âsevitanisevitaṃ.
128 Imaṃ tvaṃ tatiyaṃ tâva duḷhaṃ katvâ samâdiya
nekkhammapâramiṃ gaccha yadi bodhiṃ pattum
icchasi.
129 Yathâ andughare puriso ciravuttho dukkhaḍḍito
na tattha râgaṃ abhijaneti muttiṃ yeva gavesati.
130 Tath' eva tvaṃ sabbabhave passa andughare viya
nekkhammâbhimukho hohi bhavato parimuttiyâ.
131 Na h' ete ettakâ yeva buddhadhammâ bhavissare
aññe pi vicinissâmi ye dhammâ bhodhipâcanâ.
132 Vicinanto tadâ dakkhiṃ catutthaṃ paññâpâramiṃ
pubbakehi mahesîhi âsevitanisevitaṃ.
133 Imaṃ tvaṃ catutthaṃ tâva daḷhaṃ katvâ samâdiya

paññâpâramitaṃ gaccha yadi bodhiṃ pattum icchasi.
134 Yathâpi bhikkhu bhikkhanto hînamukkaṭṭhamajjhime
kulâni na vivajjento evaṃ labhati yâpanaṃ.
135 Tath' eva tvaṃ sabbakâlaṃ paripucchaṃ buddhaṃ janaṃ
paññâpâramitaṃ gantvâ sambodhiṃ pâpuṇissasi.
136 Na h' ete ettakâ yeva buddhadhammâ bhavissare
aññe pi vicinissâmi ye dhammâ bodhipâcanâ.
137 Vicinanto tadâ dakkhiṃ pañcamaṃ viriyapâramiṃ
pubbakehi mahesîhi âsevitanisevitaṃ.
138 Imaṃ tvaṃ pañcamaṃ tâva daḷhaṃ katvâ samâdiya
viriyapâramitaṃ gaccha yadi bodhiṃ pattum icchasi.
139 Yathâpi sîho migarâjâ nisajjaṭṭhânacaṅkame
alînaviriyo hoti paggahîtamano sadâ
140 Tath' eva tvaṃ pi sabbabhave paggaṇha viriyaṃ daḷhaṃ
viriyapâramitaṃ gantvâ sambodhiṃ pâpuṇissasi.
141 Na h' ete ettakâ yeva buddhadhammâ bhavissare
aññe pi vicinissâmi ye dhammâ bodhi-pâcanâ.
142 Vicananto tadâ dakkhiṃ chaṭṭhamaṃ khantipâramiṃ
Pubbakehi mahesîhi âsevitanisevitaṃ
143 Imaṃ tvaṃ chaṭṭhamaṃ tâva daḷhaṃ katvâ samâdiya
tattha advejjhamânaso sambodhiṃ pâpuṇissasi.
144 Yathâpi paṭhavi nâma sucim pi asucim pi ca
sabbaṃ sahati nikkhepaṃ na karoti paṭighaṃ dayaṃ.
145 Tath' eva tvaṃ pi sabbesaṃ sammânâvamânakkhamo
khantipâramitaṃ gantvâ sambodhiṃ pâpuṇissasi.
146 Na h' ete ettakâ yeva buddhadhammâ bhavissare
aññe pi vicinissâmi ye dhammâ bodhipâcanâ.
147 Vicinanto tadâ dakkhiṃ sattamaṃ saccapâramiṃ
pubbakehi mahesîhi âsevitanisevitaṃ.
148 Imaṃ tvaṃ sattamaṃ tâva daḷhaṃ katvâ samâdiya
tattha advejjhavacano sambodhiṃ pâpuṇissasi.
149 Yathâpi osadhî nâma tulâbhûtâ sadevake•
samaye utuvasse vâ na vokkamati vîthito
150 Tath' eva tvaṃ pi saccesu mâ vokkamasi vîthito
saccâpâramitaṃ katvâ sambodhiṃ pâpuṇissasi.
151 Na h' ete ettakâ yeva buddhadhammâ bhavissare
aññe pi vicinissâmi ye dhammâ bodhipâcanâ.
152 Vicinanto tadâ dakkhim aṭṭhamaṃ adhiṭṭhânapâramiṃ

pubbakehi mahesîhi âsevitanisevitaṃ
153 Imaṃ tvaṃ aṭṭhamaṃ tâva daḷhaṃ katvâ samâdiya
tattha tvaṃ acalo hutvâ sambodhiṃ pâpuṇissasi.
154 Yathâpi pabbato selo acalo suppatiṭṭhito
na kampati bhusavâtehi sakaṭṭhâne va tiṭṭhati
155 Tath' eva tvaṃ pi adhiṭṭhâne sabbadâ acalo bhava
adhiṭṭhânapâramiṃ gantvâ sambodhiṃ pâpuṇissasi.
156 Na h'ete ettakâ yeva buddhadhammâ bhavissare
aññe pi vicinissâmi ye dhammâ bodhipâcanâ.
157 Vicinanto tadâ dakkhiṃ navamaṃ mettâpâraṃ
pubbakehi mahesîhi âsevitanivesitaṃ.
158 Imaṃ tvaṃ navamaṃ tâva daḷhaṃ katvâ samâdiya
mettâya asamoho hi yadi bodhiṃ pattum icchasi.
159 Yathâpi udakaṃ nâma kalyâṇe pâpake jane
samaṃ pharati sîtena pavâheti rajomalaṃ.
160 Tath' eva tvaṃ pi hitâhite samaṃ mettâya bhâvaya
mettâpâramiṃ gantvâ sambodhiṃ pâpuṇissasi.
161 Na h'ete ettakâ yeva Buddhadhammâ bhavissare
aññe pi vicinissâmi ye dhammâ bodhipâcanâ.
162 Vicinanto tadâ dakkhiṃ dasamaṃ upekkhâpâramiṃ
pubbakehi mahesîhi âsevitanisevitaṃ.
163 Imaṃ tvaṃ dasamaṃ tâva daḷhaṃ katvâ samâdiya
tulâbhûto daḷho hutvâ sambodhiṃ pâpuṇissasi.
164 Yathâpi paṭhavî nâma nikkhittaṃ asuciṃ suciṃ
upekkhati ubho p' ete kopânunayavajjitâ.
165 Tath' eva tvaṃ pi sukhadukkhe tulâbhûto sadâ bhava
upekhâpâramitaṃ gantvâ sambodhiṃ pâpuṇissasi.
166 Ettakâ yeva te loke ye dhammâ bodhipâcanâ
tad' uddhaṃ n' atthi aññatra daḷhaṃ tattha patiṭṭhaha.
167 Ime dhamme sammasato sabhâvarasalakkhaṇe
dhammatejena vasudhâ dasasahassî pakampatha.
168 Calatî ravatî puṭhavî ucchuyantaṃ va pîḷitaṃ
telayante yathâ cakkaṃ evaṃ kampati medinî.
169 Yâvatâ parisâ âsi Buddhassa parivesane
Pavedhamânâ sâ tattha mucchitâ seti bhûmiyâ.
170 Ghaṭânekasahassâni kumbhînañca satâ bahû
sañcuṇṇamathitâ tattha aññamaññaṃ paghaṭṭitâ.
171 Ubbiggâ tasitâ bhîtâ bhantâ vyâdhitamânasâ

mahâjanâ samâgamma Dîpaṅkaram upâgamuṃ.
172 Kiṃ bhavissati lokassa kalyâṇam atha pâpakaṃ.
sabbo upadduto loko taṃ vinodehi cakkhumâ.
173 Tesaṃ tadâ saññapesi Dîpaṅkaro mahâmuni:
vissatthâ hotha mâ bhâtha imasmiṃ paṭhavikampane.
174 Yam ahaṃ ajja vyâkâsiṃ buddho loke bhavissati
eso sammasati dhammaṃ pubbakaṃ jinasevitaṃ.
175 Tassa sammasato dhammaṃ buddhabhûmiṃ asesato
tenâyaṃ kampitâ puṭhavî dasasahassî sadevake.
176 Buddhassa vacanaṃ sutvâ mano nibbâyi tâvade
sabbe maṃ upasaṃkamma puna pi maṃ abhivandiṃsu.
177 Samâdiyitvâ buddhaguṇaṃ daḷhaṃkatvâna mânasaṃ
Dîpaṅkaraṃ namassitvâ âsanâ vuṭṭhahiṃ tâdâ.
178 Dibbaṃ mânusakaṃ pupphaṃ devamânusakâ ubho
samokiranti pupphehi vuṭṭhahantassa âsanâ.
179 Vedayanti ca te sotthiṃ deva mânusakâ ubho:
mahantaṃ patthitaṃ tuyhaṃ taṃ labhassu yaṭhicchitaṃ
180 Sabbîtiyo vivajjantu sabbarogo vinassatu.
mâ te bhavantvantarâyo phusa khippaṃ bodhim uttamaṃ.
181 Yathâpi samaye patte pupphanti pupphino dumâ
tath' eva tvaṃ mahâvîra buddhañâṇena pupphasi.
182 Yathâ ye keci sambuddhâ pûrayuṃ dasapâramî
tath' eva tvaṃ mahâvîra pûraya dasapâramiṃ.
183 Yathâ ye keci sambuddhâ bodhimaṇḍamhi bujjhare
tath' eva tvaṃ mahâvîra bujjhassu jinabodhiyaṃ.
184 Yathâ ye keci sambuddhâ dhammacakkaṃ pavattayuṃ
tath' eva tvaṃ mahâvîra dhammacakkaṃ pavattaya.
185 Puṇṇamâse yathâ cando parisuddho virocati
tath' eva tvaṃ puṇṇamano viroca dasasahassiyaṃ.
186 Râhumutto yathâ suriyo tâpena atirocati
tath' eva lokâ muñcitvâ viroca siriyâ tuvaṃ.
187 Yathâ yâ kâci nadiyo osaranti mahodadhiṃ
evaṃ sadevakâ lokâ osarantu tav' antike.
188 Tehi thutippasattho so dasadhamme samâdiya
te dhamme paripûrento pavanaṃ pâvisî tadâ ti.

SUMEDHA-VATTHUKATHÂ NIṬṬHITÂ.

189 Tadâ te bhojayitvâna sasaṅghaṃ lokanâyakaṃ
upagañchuṃ saraṇaṃ tassa Dîpaṅkarassa satthuno.
190 Saraṇâgamane kañci nivesesi Tathâgato
kañci pañcasu sîlesu sîle dasavidhe paraṃ.
191 Kassaci deti sâmaññaṃ catutthe phalamuttame
kassaci asame dhamme deti so paṭisambhidâ.
192 Kassaci varasamâpattiyo aṭṭha deti narâsabho
tisso kassaci vijjâyo chaḷabhiññâ pavecchati.
193 Tena yogena janakâyaṃ ovadati mahâmuni
tena vitthârikaṃ âsi lokanâthassa sâsanaṃ.
194 Mahâhanûsabhakkhando Dîpaṅkarasanâmako
bahû jane târayati parimoceti duggatiṃ.
195 Bodhaneyyaṃ janaṃ disvâ satasahasse pi yojane
khaṇena upagantvâna bodheti taṃ mahâmuni.
196 Paṭhamâbhisamaye buddho koṭisatam abodhayi
dutiyâbhisamaye nâtho navuti koṭim abodhayi.
197 Yadâ ca devabhavanamhi buddho dhammam adesayi
navutikoṭisahassânaṃ tatiyâbhisamayo ahu.
198 Sannipâtâ tayo âsuṃ Dîpaṅkarassa satthuno:
koṭisatasahassânaṃ paṭhamo âsi samâgamo.
199 Puna Nâradakûṭamhi pavivekagate jine
khîṇâsavâ vîtamalâ samiṃsu satakoṭiyo.
200 Yamhi kâle mahâvîro Sudassanasiluccaye
navutikoṭisahassehi pavâresi mahâmuni.
201 Ahaṃ tena samayena jaṭilo uggatâpano
antalikkhamhi caraṇo pañcâbhiññâsu pâragû.
202 Dasavîsasahassânaṃ dhammâbhisamayo ahu
ekadvinnaṃ abhisamayo gaṇanâto asaṅkhiyo.
203 Vitthârikaṃ bahujaññaṃ iddhaṃ phîtaṃ ahu tadâ
Dîpaṅkarassa bhagavato sâsanaṃ suvisodhitaṃ.
204 Cattâri satasahassâni chaḷabhiññâ mahiddhikâ
Dîpaṅkaraṃ lokaviduṃ parivârenti sabbadâ.
205 Ye keci tena samayena jahanti mânusam bhavaṃ
appattamânasâ sekhâ garahitâ bhavanti te.
206 Supupphitaṃ pâvacanaṃ arahantehi tâdihi
khîṇâsavehi vimalehi upasobhati sabbadâ.
207 Nagaraṃ Rammavatî nâma Sumedho nâma khattiyo.
Sumedhâ nâma janikâ Dîpaṅkarassa satthuno.

208 Dasavassasahassâni agâraṃ ajjha so vasi
hamsâ koñcâ mayûrâ ca tayo pâsâdamuttamâ.
209 Tîṇi satasahassâni nâriyo samalaṅkatâ
Padumâ nâma sâ nârî Usabha-kkhando nâma atrajo.
210 Nimitte caturo disvâ hatthiyânena nikkhami
anûnadasamâsâni padhânaṃ padahi jino.
211 Padhânacâraṃ caretvâ abujjhi mânasaṃ muni
brahmunâ yâcito santo Dîpaṅkaro mahâmuni.
212 Vatti cakkaṃ mahâvîro Nandârâme Sirighare
nisinno sirîsamûlamhi akâ titthiyamaddanaṃ.
213 Sumaṅgalo ca Tisso ca ahesuṃ aggasâvakâ
Sâgato nâm' upaṭṭhâko Dîpaṅkarassa satthuno.
214 Nandâ c' eva Sunandâ ca ahesuṃ aggasâvikâ
bodhi tassa bhagavato pipphalî ti pavuccati
215 Tapussa-Ballikâ nâma ahesuṃ agg' upaṭṭhakâ
Sirimâ Sonâ upaṭṭhikâ Dîpaṅkarassa satthuno.
216 Asîtihatthamubbedho Dîpaṅkaro mahâmuni
sobhati Dîparukkho va Sâlarâjâ va phullito.
217 Satasahassavassâni âyu tassa mahesino
tâvatâ tiṭṭhamâno so târesi janataṃ bahuṃ.
218 Jotayitvâna saddhammaṃ santâretvâ mahâjanaṃ
jalitvâ aggikkhando va nibbuto so sasâvako.
219 Sâ ca iddhi so ca yaso tâni ca pâdesu cakkaratanâni
sabbaṃ samantarahitaṃ nanu rittâ sabbasaṅkhârâ.
220 Dîpaṅkaro jino satthâ Nandârâmamhi nibbuto
Tatth' eva tassa jina-thûpo chattiṃsubbedhayojano ti

DÎPAṄKARASSA BHAGAVATO VAṂSO PAṬHAMO.

III.

KOṆḌAÑÑA THE SECOND BUDDHA.

1 Dîpaṅkarassa aparena Koṇḍañño nâma nâyako
anantatejo amitayaso appameyyo durâsado.
2 Dharaṇûpamo so khamena sîlena sâgarûpamo
samâdhinâ Merûpamo ñâṇena gaganûpamo.
3 Indriyabalabojjhaṅgamaggasaccappakâsanaṃ
pakâsesi sadâ buddho hitâya sabbapâṇinaṃ.
4 Dhammacakkappavattente Koṇḍaññe lokanâyake
koṭisatasahassânaṃ paṭhamâbhisamayo ahu.
5 Tato param pi desente naramarûnaṃ samâgame
navutikoṭisahassânaṃ dutiyâbhisamayo ahu.
6 Titthiye abhimaddanto yadâ dhammaṃ adesayi
asîtikoṭisahassânaṃ tatiyâbhisamayo ahu.
7 Sannipâtâ tayo âsuṃ Koṇḍaññassa mahesino
khîṇâsavânaṃ vimalânaṃ santacittânaṃ tâdinaṃ.
8 Koṭisatasahassânaṃ paṭhamo âsi samâgamo
dutiyo koṭisatasahassânaṃ tatiyo navutikoṭinam.
9 Ahaṃ tena samayena Vijitâvî nâma khattiyo
samuddam antamantena isseraṃ vattayâm' ahaṃ.
10 Koṭisatasahassânaṃ vimalânaṃ mahesinaṃ
saha lokagganâthena paramannena tappayiṃ.
11 So pi maṃ buddho vyâkâsi Koṇḍañño lokanâyako
aparimeyye ito kappe buddho loke bhavissati.
12 Padhânaṃ padahitvâna katvâ dukkarakâriyaṃ
Assatthamûle sambuddho bujjhissati mahâyaso.
13 Imassa janikâ mâtâ Mâyâ nâma bhavissati
pitâ Suddhodano nâma ayaṃ hessati Gotamo.
14 Kolito Upatisso ca aggâ hessanti sâvakâ
Ânando nâm' upaṭṭhâko upaṭṭhissati maṃ jinaṃ.
15 Khemâ Uppalavaṇṇâ ca aggâ hessanti sâvikâ :
bodhi tassa bhagavato Assattho ti pavuccati.
16 Citto ca Hatthâḷavako aggâ hessant' upaṭṭhakâ
Nandamâtâ ca Uttarâ aggâ hessant' upaṭṭhikâ :

17 Âyu vassasataṃ tassa Gotamassa yasassino.
Idaṃ sutvâna vacanaṃ asamassa mahesino.
Âmoditâ naramarû buddhabîjaṅkuro ayaṃ.
18 Ukkuṭṭhisaddâ vattanti appoṭhenti hasanti ca
katañjalî namassanti dasasahassî sadevakâ.
19 Yad' imassa lokanâthassa virajjhissâma sâsanaṃ
anâgatamhi addhâne hessâma sammukhâ imaṃ.
20 Yathâ manussâ nâdiṃ tarantâ paṭititthaṃ virajjhiya
heṭṭhâ titthe gahetvâṇa uttaranti mahânadim.
21 Evam eva mayaṃ sabbe yadi muñcâm' imaṃ jinaṃ
anâgatamhi aḍdhâne hessâma sammukhâ imaṃ.
22 Tassâhaṃ vacanaṃ sutvâ bhîyyo cittam pasâdayiṃ
tam eva atthaṃ sâdhento mahârajjaṃ jine adaṃ.
mahârajjaṃ cajitvâna pabbajiṃ tassa santike.
23 Suttantaṃ vinayaṃ câpi navaṅgaṃ satthu sâsanaṃ
sabbaṃ pariyâpuṇitvâna sobhayiṃ jinasâsanaṃ.
24 Tatth' appamatto viharanto nisajjaṭṭhânacaṅkame
abhiññâpâramiṃ gantvâ brahmalokam agañch' ahaṃ.
25 Nagaraṃ Rammavatî nâma Sunando nâma khattiyo
Sujâtâ nâma janikâ Koṇḍaññassa mahesino.
26 Dasavassasahassâni agâraṃ ajjha so vasi
Ruci Suruci Subho tayo pâsâdavaramuttamâ.
27 Tîṇi satasahassâni nâriyo samalaṅkatâ
Rucidevî nâma nârî Vijitaseno nâma atrajo.
28 Nimitte caturo disvâ rathayânena nikkhami
anûnadasamâsâni padhânaṃ padahî jino.
29 Brahmunâ yâcito santo Koṇḍañño dvipaduttamo
vatti cakkaṃ mahâvîro devânam nâgaruttame.
30 Bhaddo c' eva Subhaddo ca ahesuṃ aggasâvakâ
Anuruddho nâm' upaṭṭhâko Koṇḍaññassa mahesino.
31 Tissâ ca Upatissâ ca ahesuṃ aggasâvikâ
Sâlakalyâṇikâ bodhi Koṇḍaññassa mahesino.
32 Soṇo ca Upasoṇo ca ahesuṃ aggupaṭṭhakâ
Nandâ c' eva Sirimâ ca ahesuṃ aggupaṭṭhikâ.
33 So aṭṭhâsîtihatthâni accuggato mahâmuni
Sobhati ulurâjâ va suriyo majjhantike yathâ.
34 Vassasatasahassâni âyu vijjati tâvade
tâvatâ tiṭṭhamâno so târesi janataṃ bahuṃ.

35 Khîṇâsavehi vimalehi vicittâ âsi medinî
Yathâ gaganam ulûhi evaṃ so upasobhatha.
36 Te pi nâgâ appameyyâ asaṅkhobhâ durâsadâ
vijjupâtaṃ va dassetvâ nibbutâ te mahâyasâ.
37 Sâ ca atuliyâ jinassa iddhi ñâṇa-paribhâvito samâdhi
sabbaṃ samantarahitaṃ nanu rittâ sabbasaṅkhârâ.
38 Koṇḍañño pavaro buddho Candârâmamhi nibbuto
tatth' eva cetiyo Citto sattayojanamussito ti.

KOṆḌAÑÑASSA BHAGAVATO VAṂSO DUTIYO.

IV.

MANGALA THE THIRD BUDDHA.

1 Koṇḍaññassa aparena Maṅgalo nâma ṅâyako
tamaṃ loke nihantvâna dhammokkam abhidhârayi.
2 Atulâpi pabhâ tassa jineh' aññehi uttariṃ
Candasuriyapabhaṃ hantvâ dasasahassî virocati.
3 So pi buddho pakâsesi catusaccavaruttame
te te saccarasam pîtvâ vinodenti mahâtamaṃ.
4 Patvâna bodhim atulaṃ paṭhame dhammadesane
koṭisatasahassânaṃ paṭhamâbhisamayo ahu.
5 Surindadevabhavane yadâ buddho pakâsayi
tadâ koṭisahassânaṃ dutiyâbhisamayo ahu.
6 Yadâ Sunando cakkavatti sambuddhaṃ upasaṅkami
tadâ ahani sambuddho dhammabheriṃ varuttamaṃ.
7 Sunandassânucarâ janatâ tadâsuṃ navutikoṭiyo.
sabbe pi te niravasesâ ahesuṃ ehi bhikkhukâ!
8 Sannipâtâ tayo âsuṃ Maṅgalassa mahesino
Koṭisatasahassânaṃ paṭhamo âsi samâgamo.
9 Dutiyo koṭisahassânaṃ tatiyo navuti koṭinaṃ
khîṇâsavânaṃ vimalânaṃ tadâ âsi samâgamo.
10 Ahan tena samayena Suruci nâma brâhmaṇo
ajjhâyako mantadharo tiṇṇaṃ vedânapâragû.

11 Tam ahaṃ upasaṅkamma saraṇaṃ gantvâna satthuno
sambuddhapamukhaṃ saṅghaṃ gandhamâlena pûjayiṃ.
pûjetvâ gandhamâlena gavapânena tappayiṃ.
12 So pi maṃ buddho vyâkâsi Maṅgalo dvipaduttamo
aparimeyye ito kappe ayaṃ buddho bhavissati.
13 Padhânaṃ padahitvâna katvâ dukkarakâriyaṃ
anâgatamhi addhâne hessâma sammukhâ imaṃ.
14 Tassâ pi vacanaṃ sutvâ bhîyyo cittaṃ pasâdayiṃ
uttarivataṃ adhiṭṭhâsiṃ dasapâramipûriyâ.
15 Tadâ pîtim anubrûhanto sambodhi-varapattiyâ
buddhe datvâna maṃ gehaṃ pabbajiṃ tassa santike.
16 Suttantaṃ vinayaṃ câpi navaṅgaṃ satthu sâsanaṃ
sabbaṃ pariyâpuṇitvâna sobhayiṃ jinasâsanaṃ.
17 Tatth' appamatto viharanto brahmaṃ bhâvetvâ bhâvanaṃ
abhiññâsu pâramiṃ gantvâ brahmalokaṃ agacch' ahaṃ.
18 Uttaraṃ nâma nagaraṃ Uttaro nâma khattiyo
Uttarâ nâma janikâ Maṅgalassa mahesino.
19 Navavassasahassâni agâraṃ ajjha so vasi
Yasavâ Sucimâ Sirimâ tayo pâsâdamuttamâ.
20 Samatiṃsasahassâni nâriyo samalaṅkatâ
Yasavatî nâma nârî Sîvalo nâma atrajo.
21 Nimitte caturo disvâ assayânena nikkhami
anûnakam aṭṭhamâsaṃ padhânaṃ padahi jino.
22 Brahmunâ yâcito santo Maṅgalo lokanâyako
vatti cakkaṃ mahâviro vane Sirivaruttame.
23 Sudevo Dhammaseno ca ahesuṃ aggasâvakâ
Pâlito nâm' upaṭṭhâko Maṅgalassa mahesino.
24 Sîvalâ ca Asokâ ca ahesuṃ aggasâvikâ
bodhi tassa bhagavato Nâgarukkho ti vuccati.
25 Nando c' eva Visâkho ca ahesuṃ aggupaṭṭhakâ
Anulâ c' eva Sutanâ ca ahesuṃ aggupaṭṭhikâ.
26 Aṭṭhâsîtiratanâni accugato mahâmuni
tato niddhâvati raṃsî anekasatasahassiyo.
27 Navuti vassasahassâni âyu vijjati tâvade
tâvatâ tiṭṭhamâno so târesi janataṃ bahuṃ.
28 Yathâpi sâgare ûmî na sakkâ tâ gaṇetuye
tath' eva sâvakâ tassa na sakhâ te gaṇetuye.
29 Yâvad aṭṭhâsi sambuddho Maṅgalo nâma nâyako

na tassa sâsane atthi saṅkilesamaraṇaṃ tadâ.
30 Dhammokkaṃ dhârayitvâna santâretvâ mahâjanaṃ
jalitvâ dhûmaketû va nibbuto so mahâyaso.
31 Saṅkhârânaṃ sabhâvattaṃ dassayitvâ sadevake
jalitvâ aggikkhando va suriyo atthaṅgato yathâ.
32 Uyyâne Vessaro nâma buddho nibbâyi Maṅgalo
tatth' eva tassa jina-thûpo tiṃsayojanamuggato ti.

MAṄGALASSA BHAGAVATO VAṂSO TATIYO.

V.

SUMANA THE FOURTH BUDDHA.

1 Maṅgalassa aparena Sumano nâma nâyako
sabbadhammehi asamo sabbasattânam uttamo.
2 So pi tadâ amatabherim ahani Mekhale pure
dhammasaṅkhasamâyuttaṃ navaṅgaṃ jinasâsanaṃ.
3 Jinitvâna kilese so patto sambodhim uttamaṃ
mâpesi nagaraṃ satthâ dhammapuravaruttamaṃ
4 Nirantaraṃ akutilaṃ ujuvipulavitatthataṃ.
mâpesi so mahâvîthim satipaṭṭhânavaruttamaṃ.
5 Phale cattâri sâmaññe catasso paṭisambhidâ
chaḷabhiññâ aṭṭha samâpattî pasâresi tattha vîthiyaṃ.
6 Ye appamattâ akhilâ hiriviriyeh' upâgatâ
te te ime guṇavare âdiyanti yathâ sukhaṃ.
7 Evam etena yogena uddharanto mahâjanaṃ
bodhesi paṭhamaṃ satthâ koṭisatasahassiyo.
8 Yamhi kâle mahâvîro ovadi titthiye gaṇe
koṭisahassâbhisamiṃsu dutiye dhammadesane.
9 Yadâ devâ manussâ ca samaggâ ekamânasâ
nirodhapañhaṃ pucchiṃsu saṃsayañ câpi mânasaṃ.
10 Tadâpi dhammadesane nirodhaparidîpane
navuti koṭisahassânaṃ tatiyâbhisamayo ahu.
11 Sannipâtâ tayo âsuṃ Sumanassa mahesino
khîṇâsavânaṃ vimalânaṃ santacittânaṃ tâdinaṃ.

12 Vassaṃ vuṭṭhassa bhagavato abhiguṭṭhe pavâraṇe
koṭisatasahassehi pavâresi Tathâgato.
13 Tato paraṃ sannipâte vimale Kañcanapabbate
navuti koṭisahassânaṃ dutiyo âsi samâgamo.
14 Yadâ Sakko devarâjâ buddhadassanupâgami
asîti koṭisahassânaṃ tatiyo âsi samâgamo.
15 Ahaṃ tena samayena Nâgarâjâ mahiddhiko
Atulo nâma nâmena ussannakusalapaccayo.
16 Tadâhaṃ nâgabhavanâ nikkhamitvâ sañâtihi
nâgânaṃ dibbaturiyehi sasaṅghaṃ jinam upaṭṭhahiṃ.
17 Koṭisatasahassânaṃ annapânena tappayiṃ
paccekadussayugaṃ datvâ saraṇaṃ taṃ upâgamiṃ.
18 So pi maṃ buddho vyâkâsi Sumano lokanâyako
aparimeyye ito kappe ayaṃ buddho bhavissati.
19 Padhânam padahitvâna katvâ dukkarakâriyaṃ
Anâgatamhi addhâne hessâma sammukhâ imaṃ.
20 Tassâpi vacanaṃ sutvâ bhîyyo cittaṃ pasâdayiṃ
uttarivatam adhiṭṭhâsiṃ dasapâramipûriyâ
21 Mekhalaṃ nâma nagaraṃ Sudatto nâma khattiyo
Sirimâ nâma janikâ Sumanassa mahesino.
22 Nava vassasahassâni agâraṃ ajjha so vasi
Cando Sucando Vaṭaṃso ca tayo pâsâdamuttamâ.
23 Tesaṭṭhi sahassâni nâriyo samalaṅkatâ.
Vaṭaṃsikâ nâma nârî Anupamo nâma atrajo.
24 Nimitte caturo disvâ hatthiyânena nikkhami
anûnadasamâsâni padhânaṃ padahî jino.
25 Brahmunâ yâcito santo Sumano lokanâyako
vatti cakkaṃ mahâvîro Mekhale puravuttame.
26 Saraṇo Bhâvitatto ca ahesuṃ aggasâvakâ
Udeno nâm' upaṭṭhâko Sumanassa mahesino
27 Soṇâ ca Upasoṇâ ca ahesuṃ aggasâvikâ.
so pi budho amitayaso Nâgamûle abujjhatha.
28 Varuṇo ca Saraṇo ca ahesuṃ aggupaṭṭhakâ
Câḷâ ca Upacâḷâ ca ahesuṃ aggupaṭṭhikâ.
29 Uccatarena so buddho navuti hatthasamuggato
kañcanagghiyasaṅkâso dasasahassî virocati.
30 Navuti vassasahassâni âyu vijjati tâvade
tâvatâ titthamâno so târesi janataṃ bahuṃ.

31 Târaṇîye târayitvâ bodhanîye ca bodhayi
parinibbâyi sambuddho ulurâjâ va aṭṭhami.
32 Te ca khîṇâsavâ bhikkhû so ca buddho asadiso
atulaṃ pabhaṃ dassayitvâ nibbutâ te mahâyasâ.
33 Tañ ca ñâṇam atuliyaṃ tâni c' atuliyâni ratanâni
sabbaṃ samantarahitaṃ nanu rittâ sabbasaṅkhârâ.
34 Sumano yasadharo buddho Aṅgârâmaṃhi nibbuto
tatth' eva tassa jinathûpo catuyojanam uggato ti.

SUMANASSA BHAGAVATO VAṂSO CATUTTHO.

VI.

REVATA THE FIFTH BUDDHA.

1 Sumanassa aparena Revato nâma nâyako
anupamo asadiso atulo uttamo jino.
2 So pi dhammaṃ pakâsesi Brahmunâ abhiyâcito
Khandhadhâtuvavatthânaṃ appavattaṃ bhavâbhave.
3 Tassâbhisamayâ tîṇi ahesuṃ dhammadesane
gaṇanâya na vattabbo paṭhamâbhisammayo ahu.
4 Yadâ Arindamaṃ râjaṃ vinesi Revato muni
tadâ koṭisatasahassânaṃ dutiyâbhisamayo ahu.
5 Sattâhaṃ paṭisallânâ vuṭṭhahitvâ narâsabho
Koṭisataṃ naramarûnaṃ vinesi uttame phale.
6 Sannipâtâ tayo âsuṃ Revatassa mahesino
Khîṇâsavânaṃ vimalânaṃ suvimuttânaṃ tâdinaṃ.
7 Atikkantâ gaṇanapathâ paṭhamâ ye samâgatâ
Koṭisatasahassânaṃ dutiyo âsi samâgamo.
8 Yo so paññâya asamo tassa cakkânuvattako
So tadâ vyâdhito âsi patto jîvitasaṃsayaṃ
9 Tassa gilânapucchâya ye tadâ upagatâ muni
Koṭisatasahassâ arahanto tatiyo âsi samâgamo.
10 Ahaṃ tena samayena Atidevo nâma brâhmaṇo.
upagantvâ Revataṃ buddhaṃ saraṇaṃ tassagacch' ahaṃ
11 Tassa sîlaṃ samâdhiñ ca paññâguṇavaruttamaṃ
thomayitvâ yathâ thomaṃ uttarîyam adâs' ahaṃ.

12 So pi maṃ buddho vyâkâsi Revato lokanâyako
aparimeyye ito kappe ayaṃ buddho bhavissati:
13 Padhânaṃ padahitvâna katvâ dukkarakâriyaṃ
Anâgatamhi addhâne hessâma sammukhâ imaṃ.
14 Tassâpi vacanaṃ sutvâ bhîyyo cittaṃ pasâdayi
uttarivatam adhiṭṭhâsiṃ dasapâramipûriyâ.
15 Tadâ pi taṃ buddha dhammaṃ saritvâ anubrûhayiṃ
âharissâmi taṃ dhammaṃ yaṃ mayhaṃ abhipatthitaṃ.
16 Nagaraṃ Sudhaññakaṃ nâma Vipulo nâma khattiyo
Vipulâ nâma janikâ Revatassa mahesino.
17 Chabbassasataṃsahassâni agâraṃ ajjha so vasi
Sudassano ca ratanagghi Avelo ca vibhûsito:
Puññakammâbhinibbattâ tayo pâsâdamuttamâ.
18 Tettiṃsa-sahassâni nâriyo samalaṅkatâ
Sudassanâ nâma devî Varuṇo nâma atrajo.
19 Nimitte caturo disvâ rathayânena nikkhami
anûnasattamâsâni padhânam padahi jino.
20 Brahmunâ yâcito santo Revato lokanâyako
vatti cakkaṃ mahâvîro Varuṇârâme Sirighaṇe.
21 Varuṇo Brahmadevo ca ahesuṃ aggasâvakâ
Sambhavo nâm' upaṭṭhâko Revatassa mahesino.
22 Bhaddâ c' eva Subhaddâ ca ahesuṃ aggasâvikâ
so pi buddho asamasamo Nâgamûle abujjhatha.
23 Padumo, Kuñjaro c' eva ahesuṃ aggupaṭṭhakâ
Sirimâ c' eva Yasavatî ahesuṃ aggupaṭṭhikâ.
24 Uccatarena so buddho asîtihatthamuggato.
obhâseti disâ sabbâ indaketu va uggato.
25 Tassa sarîre nibbattâ pabhâmâlâ anuttarâ
dîvâ vâ yadi vâ rattiṃ samantâ phari yojanaṃ.
26 Saṭṭhi vassasahassâni âyu vijjati tâvade
tâvatâ tiṭṭhamâno so târesi janataṃ bahuṃ.
27 Dassayitvâ buddhabalaṃ amataṃ loke pakâsayaṃ
nibbâyi anupâdâno yathaggupâdânasaṅkhayâ.
28 So ca kâyo ratananibho so ca dhammo asâdiso
sabbaṃ samantarahitaṃ nanu rittâ sabbasaṅkhârâ.
29 Revato yasadharo buddho nibbuto so mahâmuni
dhâtuvitthârikaṃ âsi tesu tesu padesato ti.

REVATASSA BHAGAVATO VAṂSO PAÑCAMO.

VII.

SOBHITA THE SIXTH BUDDHA.

1 Revatassa aparena Sobhito nâma nâyako
samâhito *santacitto asamo appaṭipuggalo.*
2 So jino *sakagehamhi mânasaṃ vinivattayi*
patvâna kevalaṃ *bodhiṃ dhammacakkaṃ pavattayi.*
3 Yâva uddhaṃ *avîcito bhavaggâ câpi heṭṭhato*
etth' antare ekaparisâ *ahosi dhammadesane.*
4 Tâya parisâya sambuddho dhammacakkaṃ pavattayi
gaṇanâya na vattabbo paṭhamâbhisamayo ahu.
5 Tato param pi desente naramarûnaṃ samâgame
nuvati koṭisahassânaṃ dutiyâbhisamayo ahu.
6 Punâparaṃ râjaputto Jayaseno nâma khattiyo
ârâmaṃ ropayitvâna buddhe nîyâtayi tadâ.
7 Tassa yogaṃ pakittento dhammaṃ desesi cakkhumâ
tâdâ koṭisahassânaṃ tatiyâbhisamayo ahu.
8 Sannipâtâ tayo âsuṃ Sobhitassa mahesino
khîṇâsavânaṃ vimalânaṃ santacittânaṃ tâdinaṃ.
9 Uggato nâma so rajâ dânaṃ deti naruttame
tamhi dâne samâgañchuṃ arahantâ satakoṭiyo.
10 Punâparaṃ puragaṇo dânaṃ deti naruttame
tadâ navutikoṭînaṃ dutiyo âsi samâgamo.
11 Devaloke vasitvâna yahâ orohati jino
tadâ asîtikoṭînaṃ tatiyo âsi samâgamo.
12 Ahaṃ tena samayena Sujâto nâma brâhmaṇo
tadâ sasâvakaṃ buddhaṃ annapânena tappayiṃ.
13 So pi maṃ buddho vyâkâsi Sobhito lokanâyako
aparimeyye ito kappe ayaṃ buddho bhavissati.
14 Padhânaṃ padahitvâno . . . pe . . . [iv. 13]
. . . pe . . . hessâma sammukhâ imaṃ.
15 Tassâ pi vacanaṃ sutvâ haṭṭho saṃviggamânaso
tam ev' attham anupattiyâ uggaṃ dhitim akâs' ahaṃ.
16 Sudhammaṃ nagaraṃ Sudhammo nâma khattiyo
Sudhammâ nâmá janikâ Sobhitassa mahesino.

17 Nava vassasahassânaṃ agâraṃ ajjha so vasi
Kumudo Naḷiro Padumo tayo pâsâdamuttamâ.
18 Asattati sahassâni nariyo samalaṅkatâ
Samaṅgî nâma sâ nârî Sîho nâm' âsi atrajo.
19 Nimitte caturo disvâ pâsâdenâbhinikkhami
sattâhaṃ padhânacâraṃ caritvâ purisuttamo.
20 Brahmunâ yâcito santo Sobhito lokanâyako
Vatti cakkaṃ mahâvîro Sudhamm' uyyânamuttame.
21 Asamo ca Sunetto ca ahesuṃ aggasâvakâ
Anumo nâm' upaṭṭhâko Sobhitassa mahesino.
22 Nakulâ ca Sujâtâ ca ahesuṃ aggasâvikâ
bujjhamâno ca so buddho Nâgamûle abujjhatha.
23 Rammo c' eva Sudatto ca ahesuṃ aggupaṭṭhakâ
Nakulâ c' eva Cittâ ca ahesuṃ aggupaṭṭhikâ.
24 Aṭṭhapaññâsaratanaṃ accuggato mahâmuni
obhâseti disâ sabbâ sataraṃsî va uggato.
25 Yathâ suphullaṃ pavanaṃ nânâgandhehi dhûpitaṃ
tath' eva tassa pâvacanaṃ sîlagandhehi dhûpitaṃ.
26 Yathâpi sâgaro nâma dassanena atappiyo
tath' eva tassa pâvacanaṃ savanena atappiyaṃ.
27 Navutivassasahassâni âyu vijjati tâvade
tâvatâ tiṭṭhamâno so târesi janataṃ bahuṃ.
28 Ovâdaṃ anusiṭṭhiñ ca datvâna sesake jane
hutâsano va tâpetvâ nibbuto so sasâvako.
29 So ca buddho asamasamo te pi ca sâvakâ balappattâ
sabbaṃ samantarahitaṃ nanu rittâ sabbasaṅkhârâ.
30 Sobhito varasambuddho Sîhârâmamhi nibbuto
dhâtuvittharikaṃ âsi tesu tesu padesato ti.

SOBHITASSA BHAGAVATO VAṂSO CHAṬṬHAMO.

VIII.

ANOMADASSI THE SEVENTH BUDDHA.

1 Sobhitassa aparena sambuddho dvipaduttamo
Anomadassî amitayaso tejasî duratikkamo.
2 So chetvâ bandhanaṃ sabbaṃ vidhaṃsetvâ tayo bhave
anivatti-gamanaṃ maggaṃ desesi devamânuse.
3 Sâgaro va asaṅkhobho pabbato va durâsado
Âkâso va ananto so Sâlarâjâ va phullito.
4 Dassanena pi taṃ buddhaṃ tositâ honti pâṇino
vyâharantaṃ giraṃ sutvâ amataṃ pâpuṇanti te.
5 Dhammâbhisamayo tassa iddho phîto tadâ ahu:
koṭisatâni abhisamiṃsu paṭhame dhammadesane.
6 Tato param pi abhisamaye vassante dhammavuṭṭhiyo
asîtikoṭiyo abhisamiṃsu dutiye dhammadesane.
7 Tato param pi vassante tappayante ca pâṇinaṃ
aṭṭhasattati koṭînaṃ tatiyâbhisamayo ahu.
8 Sannipâtâ tayo âsum tassâpi ca mahesino
abhiññâbalappattânaṃ pupphitânaṃ vimuttiyâ.
9 Aṭṭha satasahassânaṃ sannipâtâ tadâ ahu
pahînamadamohânaṃ santacittânaṃ tâdinaṃ.
10 Sattasatasahassânaṃ dutiyâsi samâgamo
anaṅganânaṃ virajânaṃ upasantânaṃ tâdinaṃ.
11 Channaṃ satasahassânaṃ tatiyo âsi samâgamo
abhiññâbalappattânaṃ nibbutânaṃ tappassinaṃ.
12 Ahaṃ tena samayena yakkho âsi mahiddhiko
nekânaṃ yakkhakoṭînaṃ Vasavattiṃhi issaro.
13 Tadâpi taṃ buddhavaraṃ upagantvâ mahesinaṃ
annapânena tappesiṃ sasaṅghaṃ lokanâyakaṃ.
14 So pi maṃ tadâ vyâkâsi visuddhanayano muni
aparimeyye ito kappe ayaṃ buddho bhavissati.
15 Padhânaṃ padahitvâna . . . pe . . . [iv. 13]
. . . pe . . . hessâma sammukhâ imaṃ.
16 Tassâ pi vacanaṃ sutvâ haṭṭho saṃviggamânaso
uttarivatam addhiṭṭhâsiṃ dasapâramipûriyâ.

17 Nagaraṃ Candavatî nâma Yasavâ nâma khattiyo
mâtâ Yasodharâ nâma Anomadassissa satthuno.
18 Dasavasasahassâni agâraṃ ajjha so vasi
Siri Upasiri Vaḍḍho tayo pâsâdamuttamâ.
19 Tevîsatisahassâni nâriyo samalaṅkatâ
Sirimâ nâma nârî ca Upavâno nâma atrajo.
20 Nimitte caturo disvâ sivikâyâbhinikkhami
anûnadasamâsâni padhânaṃ padahi jino.
21 Brahmunâ yâcito santo Anomadassî mahâmuni
vatti cakkaṃ mahâvîro uyyâne so Sudassane.
22 Nisabho ca Asoko ca ahesuṃ aggasâvakâ
Varuṇo nâm'upaṭṭhâko Anomadassissa satthuno.
23 Sundarî ca Sumanâ ca ahesuṃ aggasâvikâ
bodhi tassa bhagavato Ajjuno ti pavuccati.
24 Nandivaḍḍho Sirivaḍḍho ahesuṃ aggupaṭṭhakâ
Uppalâ c' eva Padumâ ca ahesuṃ aggupaṭṭhikâ.
25 Aṭṭhapaññâsaratanaṃ accuggato mahâmuni
pabhâ niddhâvati tassa sataraṃsî va uggato.
26 Vasasatasahassâni âyu vijjati tâvade
tâvatâ tiṭṭhamâno so târesi janataṃ bahuṃ.
27 Supupphitaṃ pâvacanaṃ arahantehi tâdihi
vîtarâgehi vimalehi sobhittha jina-sâsanaṃ.
28 So ca satthâ amitayaso yugâni tâni atuliyâni
sabbaṃ samantarahitaṃ nanu rittâ sabbasaṅkhârâ.
29 Anomadassî jino satthâ Dhammârâmamhi nibbuto
tath' eva tassa jinathûpo ubbedho paññavîsatî ti.

ANOMADASSISSA BHAGAVATO VAṂSO SATTAMO.

IX.

PADUMA THE EIGHTH BUDDHA.

1 Anomadassissa aparena sambuddho dvipaduttamo
Padumo nâma nâmena asamo appaṭipuggalo.
2 Tassâpi asamaṃ sîlaṃ samâdhi pi anantakâ
asaṅkheyyaṃ ñâṇavaraṃ vimutti pi anupamâ.
3 Tassâ pi atulatejassa dhammacakkappavattane
abhisamayâ tayo âsuṃ mahâtamapavâhanâ.
4 Paṭhamâbhisamaye buddho koṭisatam abodhayi
dutiyâbhisamaye dhîro navuti koṭiṃ abodhayi.
5 Yadâ ca Padumo buddho ovadi sakaṃ atrajaṃ
tadâ asîtikoṭînaṃ tatiyâbhisamayo ahu.
6 Sannipâtâ tayo âsuṃ Padumassa mahesino
koṭisatasahassânaṃ paṭhamo âsi samâgamo.
7 Kaṭhinatthârasamaye uppanne kaṭhinacîvare
dhamma senâpatatthâya bhikkhû sibbiṃsu cîvaraṃ.
8 Tadâ te vimalâ bhikkhû chaḷabhiññâ mahiddhikâ
tîṇi satasahassâni samiṃsu aparâjitâ.
9 Punâparaṃ so narâsabho pavane vâsaṃ upâgami
tadâ samâgamo âsi dvinnaṃ satasahassânaṃ.
10 Ahaṃ tena samayena sîho âsiṃ migâdhibhû
vivekam anubrûhantaṃ pavane addasaṃ jinaṃ.
11 Vanditvâ sirasâ pâde katvâna tam padakkhiṇaṃ
tikkhattuṃ abhinanditvâ sattâhaṃ jinaṃ upaṭṭhahiṃ.
12 Sattâhaṃ varasamâpattiyâ vuṭṭhahitvâ Tathâgato
manasâ cintayitvâna koṭibhikkhû samânayi.
13 Tadâpi so mahâvîro tesaṃ majjhe viyâkari
aparimeyye ito kappe ayaṃ buddho bhavissati
14 Padhânaṃ padahitvâna . . . pe . . . [vi. 13]
. . . pe . . . hessâma sammukhâ imaṃ.
15 Tassâpi vacanaṃ sutvâ bhîyyo cittam pasâdayi
Uttarivatam adhiṭṭhâsim dasapâramipûriyâ
16 Campakaṃ nâma nagaraṃ Asamo nâmo khattiyo
Asamâ nâma janikâ Padumassa mahesino.

17 Dasavassasahassâni agâraṃ ajjha so vasi
Nandâ ca Suyasâ Uttarâ tayo pâsâdamuttamâ.
18 Tettiṃsasatasahassâni nâriyo samalaṅkatâ
Uttarâ nâma sâ nârî Rammo nâm' âsi atrajo.
19 Nimitte caturo disvâ rathayânena nikkhami
anûnakaṃ aḍḍhamâsaṃ padhânaṃ padahi jino.
20 Brahmunâ yâcito santo Padumo lokanâyako
Vatti cakkaṃ mahâvîro Dhanañjuyyânamuttame
21 Sâlo ca Upasâlo ca ahesuṃ aggasâvakâ
Varuṇo nâm' upaṭṭhâko Padumassa mahesino.
22 Râdhâ c' eva Surâdhâ ca ahesuṃ aggasâvikâ
bodhi tâssa bhagavato Mahâsoṇo ti vuccati.
23 Bhîyyo c' eva Asamo ca ahesuṃ aggupaṭṭhakâ
Rucî ca Nandarâmâ ca ahesuṃ aggupaṭṭhikâ.
24 Aṭṭhapaññâsaratanaṃ accugato mahâmuni
pabhâ niddhâvati tassa asamâ sabbaso disâ.
25 Candappabhâ suriyappabhâ ratanagghimaṇippabhâ
sabbâ pitâhatâ honti patvâ jinappabhuttamaṃ.
26 Vassasatasahassâni âyu vijjati tâvade
tâvatâ tiṭṭhamâno so târesi janataṃ bahuṃ.
27 Paripakkamânase satte bodhayitvâ asesato
sesake anusâsetvâ nibbuto so sasâvako.
28 Urago va tacaṃ jiṇṇaṃ vuḍḍhaṃ pattaṃ va pâdapo
jahitvâ sabbasaṅkhâre nibbuto so yathâ sikhî ti.
29 Padumo jinavaro satthâ Dhammâramamhi nibbuto
dhâtuvitthârikaṃ âsi tesu tesu padesato ti.

PADUMASSA BHAGAVATO VAṂSO AṬṬHAMO.

X.

NÂRADA THE NINTH BUDDHA.

1 Padumassa aparena sambuddho dvipaduttamo
Nârado nâma nâmena asamo appaṭipuggalo.
2 So buddho cakkavattissa jeṭṭho dayita-oraso
âmuttamalyâbharaṇo uyyânaṃ upasaṅkami.
3 Tatrâsi rukkho yasavipulo abhirûpo brahmâsuci
taṃ ajjhapatvâ nisîdi Mahâsoṇassa heṭṭhato.
4 Tassa ñâṇavar' uppajji anantaṃ vajirûpamaṃ
tena vicini saṅkhâre ukujjaṃ avakujjakaṃ.
5 Tattha sabbakilesâni asesaṃ abhivâhayi
pâpuṇi kevalaṃ bodhiṃ buddhañâṇañ ca cuddasaṃ.
6 Pâpuṇitvâna sambodhiṃ dhammacakkaṃ pavattayi
koṭisatasahassânaṃ paṭhamâbhisamayo ahu.
7 Mahâdonaṃ nâgarâjaṃ vinayanto mahâmuni
pâṭiheraṃ tadâkâsi dassayanto sadevake.
8 Tadâ devamanussânaṃ tamhi dhammapakâsane
navuti koṭisahassânaṃ tariṃsu sabbasaṃsayaṃ.
9 Yamhi kâle mahâvîro ovadi sakaṃ atrajaṃ
asîti koṭisahassânaṃ tatiyâbhisamayo ahu.
10 Sannipâtâ tayo âsuṃ Nâradassa mahesino
koṭisatasahassâni paṭhamo âsi samâgamo.
11 Yadâ buddho buddhaguṇaṃ sanidânaṃ pakâsayi
navuti koṭisahassânaṃ samiṃsu vimalâ tadâ.
12 Yadâ Verocano nâgo dânaṃ dadâti satthuno
tadâ samiṃsu jinaputtâ asîtisatasahassiyo.
13 Ahaṃ tena samayena jaṭilo uggatâpano
antalikkha-caro âsiṃ pañcâbhiññâsu pâragû.
14 Tadâ pâham asamasamaṃ sasaṅghaṃ saparijanaṃ
annapânena tappetvâ candanenâbhipûjayiṃ.
15 So pi maṃ tadâ vyâkâsi Nârado lokanâyako
aparimeyye ito kappe ayaṃ buddho bhavissati.
16 Padhânaṃ padahitvâna . . . pe . . . [iv. 13]
. . . pe . . . hessâma sammukhâ imaṃ.

17 Tassâpi vacanaṃ sutvâ bhîyyo hâsetvâ mânasaṃ
adhiṭṭhahiṃ vataṃ uggaṃ dasapâramipûriyâ.
18 Nagaraṃ Dhaññavatî nâma Sudevo nâma khattiyo
Anomâ nâma janikâ Nâradassa mahesino.
19 Nava vassasahassâni agâraṃ ajjha so vasi
Jitâvijitâbhirâmâ tayo pâsâdamuttamâ.
20 Ticattârîsasahassâni nâriyo samalaṅkatâ
Jitasenâ nâma nârî Nanduttaro nâma atrajo.
21 Nimitte caturo disvâ padasâ gamanena nikkhami
sattâhaṃ padhânacâriyaṃ acari lokanâyako.
22 Brahmunâ yâcito santo Nârado lokanâyako
vatti cakkaṃ mahâvîro Dhanañjuyyânamuttame.
23 Bhaddasâlo Jitamitto ahesuṃ aggasâvakâ
Vâseṭṭho nâm' upaṭṭhâko Nâradassa mahesino.
24 Uttarâ Phaggunî c' eva ahesuṃ aggasâvikâ
bodhi tassa bhagavato Mahâsoṇo ti vuccati.
25 Uggarindo Vasabho ca ahesuṃ aggupaṭṭhakâ
Indavarî ca Caṇḍî ca ahesuṃ aggupaṭṭhikâ.
26 Aṭṭhâsîtiratanâni accugato mahâmuni
kañcanagghikasaṅkâso dasasahassî virocatha.
27 Tassa byâmappabhâ kâyâ niddhâvanti disodisaṃ
nirantaraṃ divâ rattiṃ yojanaṃ pharate disâ.
28 Na keci tena samayena samantâ yojane janâ
ukkâ padîpe ujjalenti buddharaṃsena otthatâ.
29 Navutivassasahassâni âyu vijjati tâvade
tâvatâ tiṭṭhamâno so târesi janataṃ bahuṃ.
30 Yathâ uḷubhigaganaṃ vicittaṃ upasobhati
tath' eva sâsanaṃ tassa arantehi sobhati.
31 Saṃsârasotaṃ taraṇâya sesake paṭipannake
dhammasetuṃ daḷhaṃ katvâ nibbuto so narâsabho.
32 So pi buddho asamasamo te pi khîṇâsavâ atulatejâ
sabbaṃ samantarahitaṃ nanu rittâ sabbasaṅkhârâ.
33 Nârado jinavasabho nibbuto Sudassane pure
tatth' eva jinathûpavaro catuyojanam uggato ti.

NÂRADASSA BHAGAVATO VAṂSO NAVAMO.

XI.

PADUMUTTARA THE TENTH BUDDHA.

1 Nâradassa aparena sambuddho dvipaduttamo
Padumattaro nâma jino akkhobbho sâgarûpamo.
2 Maṇḍakappo va so âsi yamhi buddho ajâyatha
ussannakusalâ janatâ tamhi kappe ajâyatha.
3 Padumuttarassa bhagavato paṭhame dhammadesane
Koṭisatasahassânaṃ dhammâbhisamayo ahu.
4 Tato param hi vassante tappayante ca pâṇine
sattatiṃsasahassânaṃ dutiyâbhisamayo ahu.
5 Yamhi kâle mahâvîro Ânandaṃ upasaṅkami
pitu santikaṃ upagantvâ ahani amatadudrabhiṃ
6 Ahate dhammabherimhi vassante dhammavuṭṭhiyo
paññâsasatasahassânaṃ tatiyâbhisamayo ahu.
7 Ovâdako viññâpako târako sabbapâṇinaṃ
desanâkusalo buddho târesi janataṃ bahuṃ.
8 Sannipâtâ tayo âsuṃ Padumattarassa satthuno
koṭisatasahassânaṃ paṭhamo âsi samâgamo.
9 Yadâ buddho asamasamo vasati Vebhârapabbate
navutikoṭisahassânaṃ dutiyo âsi samâgamo.
10 Puna cârikaṃ pakkante gâmanigamaraṭṭhato
asîtikotisahassânaṃ tatiyo âsi samâgamo.
11 Ahaṃ tena samayena jatiḷo nâma Raṭṭhiko
Sambuddhapamukhaṃ saṅghaṃ sabhattadussam adâs' ahaṃ.
12 So pi maṃ buddho vyâkâsi saṅghamajjhe nisîdiya
satasahasse ito kappe ayaṃ buddho bhavissati.
13 Padhânaṃ padahitvâna . . . pe . . . [iv. 13]
. . . pe . . . hessâma sammukhâ imaṃ.
14 Tassâpi vacanaṃ sutvâ uttarivataṃ adhiṭṭhahiṃ
akâsi maggaṃ daḷhaṃ dhitim dasapâramipûriyâ.
15 Vyâhatâ titthiyâ sabbe vimanâ dummanâ tadâ
na tesaṃ keci paricaranti raṭṭhato nicchubhanti te.

16 Sabbe tattha samâgantvâ upagacchuṃ buddhasantike
tuvaṃ nâtho mahâvîra saraṇaṃ hohi cakkhumâ!
17 Anukampako kâruṇiko hite si sabbapâṇinaṃ
sampatte titthiye sabbe pañca sîle patiṭṭhahi!
18 Evaṃ nirâkulaṃ âsi suññataṃ titthiyehi taṃ
vicittaṃ arahantehi vasibhûtehi tâdihi!
19 Nagaraṃ Haṃsavatî nâma Ânando nâma khattiyo
Sujâtâ nâma janikâ Padumuttarassa mahesino.
20 Dasavassasahassâni agâraṃ ajjha so vasi
Nâravâhano Yaso Vasavatti tayo pâsâdamuttamâ.
21 Ticattârimsasahassâni nâriyo samalaṅkatâ
Vasudattâ nâma nârî Uttaro nâma atrajo.
22 Nimitte caturo disvâ pâsâdenâbhinikkhami
sattâhaṃ padhânacâraṃ acari purisuttamo.
23 Brahmunâ yâcito santo Padumuttaro vinâyako
vatti cakkaṃ mahavîro Mithiluyyânamuttame.
24 Devalo ca Sujâto ca ahesuṃ aggasâvakâ
Sumano nâm' upaṭṭhâko Padumuttarassa mahesino.
25 Amitâ Asamâ c' eva ahesuṃ aggasâvikâ
bodhi tassa bhagavato Salaḷo ti pavuccati.
26 Vitiṇṇo c' eva Tisso ca ahesuṃ aggupaṭṭhakâ
Hatthâ c' eva Vicittâ ca ahesuṃ aggupaṭṭhikâ.
27 Aṭṭhapaññâsaratanaṃ accugato mahâmuni
kañcanagghikasaṃkâso dvattiṃsavaralakkhaṇo.
28 Kuṭṭâkavâṭâ bhitti ca rukkhâ naga-siluccayâ
na tassâvaraṇâ atthi samantâ dvâdasayojane.
29 Vassasatasahassâni âyu vijjati tâvade
tâvatâ tiṭṭhamâno so târesi janataṃ bahuṃ.
30 Santâretvâ bahujanaṃ chindetvâ sabbasaṃsayaṃ
jalitvâ aggikkhandho va nibbuto so sasâvako.
31 Padumuttaro jino buddho Nandârâmamhi nibbuto
tatth' eva tassa thûpavaro dvâdasubbedhayojano ti.

PADUMUTTARASSA BHAGAVATO VAṂSO DASAMO.

XII.

SUMEDHA THE ELEVENTH BUDDHA.

1 Padumuttarassa aparena Sumedho nâma nâyako
durâsado uggatejo sabbalokuttaro muni.
2 Pasannanetto sumukho brahâ ujupatâpavâ
hite si sabbasattânaṃ bahû mocesi bandhanâ.
3 Yadâ buddho pâpuṇitvâ kevalaṃ bodhim uttamaṃ
Sudassanamhi nagare dhammacakkam pavattayi.
4 Tassâbhisamayâ tiṇi ahesuṃ dhammadesane
koṭisatasahassânaṃ paṭhamâbhisamayo ahu.
5 Punâparaṃ kumbhakaṇṇaṃ yakkhaṃ so damayi jino
navutikoṭisahassânaṃ dutiyâbhisamayo ahu.
6 Punâparaṃ amitayaso catusaccaṃ pakâsayi
asîtikoṭisahassânaṃ tatiyâbhisamayo ahu.
7 Sannipâtâ tayo âsuṃ Sumedhassa mahesino
khînâsavânaṃ vimalânaṃ santa cittânaṃ tâdinaṃ.
8 Sudassanaṃ nagaraṃ varaṃ upagacchi jino yadâ
tadâ khîṇâsavâ bhikkhû samiṃsu satakoṭiyo.
9 Punâparaṃ Devakûṭe bhikkhûnaṃ kathiṇatthate
tadâ navutikoṭînaṃ dutiyo âsi samâgamo.
10 Punâparaṃ dasabalo yadâ carati cârikaṃ
tadâ asîtikoṭînaṃ tatiyo âsi samâgamo.
11 Ahaṃ tena samayena Uttaro nâma mâṇavo
asîtikoṭiyo mayhaṃ ghare sannicittaṃ dhanaṃ.
12 Kevalaṃ sabbaṃ datvâna sasaṅghaṃ lokanâyakaṃ
saraṇaṃ tass' upâgacchiṃ pabbajjañ câbhirocayi.
13 So pi maṃ buddho vyâkâsi karonto anumodanaṃ
tiṃsakappasahassamhi ayaṃ buddho bhavissati.
14 Padhânaṃ padahitvâna . . . pe . . . [iv. 13]
. . . pe . . . hessâma sammukhâ imaṃ.
15 Tassâpi vacanaṃ sutvâ bhîyyo cittaṃ pasâdayi
uttarivataṃ adhiṭṭhâsiṃ dasapâramipûriyâ.
16 Suttantaṃ vinayaṃ câpi navaṅgaṃ satthusâsanaṃ
sabbaṃ pariyâpuṇitvâna sobhayi jinasâsanaṃ

17 Tatth' appamatto viharanto nisajjaṭṭhânacaṅkame
abhiññâsu pâramiṃ gantvâ brahmalokaṃ agacch' ahaṃ.
18 Sudassanaṃ nâma nagaraṃ Sudatto nâma khattiyo
Sudattâ nâma janikâ Sumedhassa mahesino.
19 Navavassasahassâni agâraṃ ajjha so vasi
Sucanda-kañcana-sirivaḍḍhâ tayo pâsâdamuttamâ.
20 Tisoḷasasahassâni nâriyo samalaṅkatâ
Sumanâ nâma sâ nârî Sumitto nâma atrajo.
21 Nimitte caturo disvâ hatthi-yânena nikkhami
anûnakaṃ aḍḍhamâsaṃ padhânaṃ padahi jino.
22 Brahmunâ yâcito santo Sumedho lokanâyako
Vatti cakkaṃ mahâvîro Sudassanuyyânamuttame
23 Saraṇo Sabbakâmo ca ahesuṃ aggasâvakâ
Sâgaro nâm' upaṭṭhâko Sumedhassa mahesino.
24 Râmâ c' eva Surâmâ ca ahesuṃ aggasâvikâ
bodhi tassa bhagavato Mahânimbo ti vuccati.
25 Uruveḷo ca Yasavo ca ahesuṃ aggupaṭṭhakâ
Yasodharâ Sirimâ ca ahesuṃ aggupaṭṭhikâ.
26 Aṭṭhâsîtiratanâni accuggato mahâmuni
Obhâseti disâ sabbâ cando târagaṇe yathâ.
27 Cakkavattimaṇi nâma yathâ tapati yojanaṃ
tath' eva tassa ratanaṃ samantâ pharati yojanaṃ.
28 Navutivassasahassâni âyu vijjati tâvade
tâvatâ tiṭṭhamâno so târesi janataṃ bahuṃ.
29 Tevijjâchaḷabhiññehi balappattehi tâdihi
Samâkulam idaṃ âsi arahantehi tâdihi.
30 Te pi sabbe amitayasâ vippamuttâ nirûpadhî
ñâṇâlokaṃ dassayitvâ nibbutâ te mahâyasâ.
31 Sumedho jinavaro buddho Medhârâmamhi nibbuto
dhâtuvitthârikam âsi tesu tesu padesato ti.

SUMEDHASSA BHAGAVATO VAṂSO EKÂDASAMO.

XIII.

SUJÂTA THE TWELFTH BUDDHA.

1 Tatth' eva Maṇḍakappamhi Sujâto nâma nâyako
sîhahanu-usabhakkhandho appameyyo durâsado.
2 Cando va vimalo suddho sataraṃsi va tâpavâ
evaṃ sobhati sambuddho jalanto siriyâ pabhâ.
3 Papuṇitvâna sambuddho kevalaṃ bodhim uttamaṃ
Sumaṅgalamhi nagare dhammacakkaṃ pavattayi.
4 Desente pavaraṃ dhammaṃ Sujâte lokanâyake
asîtikoṭî abhisamiṃsu paṭhame dhammadesane.
5 Yadâ Sujâto amitayaso deve vassaṃ upâgami
sattatiṃsasahassânaṃ dutiyâbhisamayo ahu.
6 Yadâ Sujâto asamasamo upagacchi pitu santikaṃ
saṭṭhisatasahassânaṃ tatiyâbhisamayo ahu.
7 Sannipâtâ tayo âsuṃ Sujâtassa mahesino
khîṇâsavânaṃ vimalânaṃ santacittânaṃ tâdinaṃ.
8 Abhiññâbalappattânaṃ appattânaṃ bhavâbhave
Saṭṭhi satasahassânaṃ paṭhamaṃ sannipatiṃsu te.
9 Punâparaṃ sannipâte tidivorohane jine
paññâsa satasahassânaṃ dutiyo âsi samâgamo.
10 Upasaṇkamanto naravasabhaṃ tassa yo aggasâvako
catûhi satasahassehi sambuddhaṃ upasaṅkami.
11 Ahaṃ tena samayena catudîpamhi issaro
antalikkhacaro âsi cakkavattî mahabbalo.
12 Loke acchariyaṃ disvâ abbhutaṃ lomahaṃsanaṃ
upagantvâna vandayiṃ Sujâtaṃ lokanâyakam.
13 Catudîpe mahârajjaṃ ratane sattauttame
buddhe nîyâdayitvâna pabbaji tassa santike.
14 Arâmikâ janapade uṭṭhânaṃ paṭipiṇḍiyam
upanenti bhikkhusaṅghassa paccayaṃ sayanâsanaṃ.
15 So pi maṃ buddho vyâkâsi dasasahassamhi issaro
tiṃse kappasahassamhi ayaṃ buddho bhavissati.

16 Padhânaṃ padahitvâna . . . pe . . . [iv. 13]
. . . pe . . . hessâma sammukhâ imaṃ.
17 Tassâpi vacanaṃ sutvâ bhîyyo hâsaṃ jane sahaṃ
adhiṭṭhahiṃ vataṃ uggaṃ dasapâramipûriyâ.
18 Suttantaṃ vinayañ câpi navaṅgaṃ satthasâsanaṃ
sabbaṃ pariyâpuṇitvâna sobhayiṃ jinasâsanaṃ.
19 Tatth' appamatto viharanto brahmaṃ bhâvetvâ bhâvanaṃ
abhiññâsu pâramiṃ gantvâ brahmalokaṃ agacch' ahaṃ.
20 Sumaṅgalaṃ nâma nagaraṃ Uggato nâma khattiyo
mâtâ Pabbâvatî nâma Sujâtassa mahesino.
21 Navavassasahassâni agâraṃ ajjha so vasi
Siri Upasiri Nandâ tayo pâsâdamuttamâ.
22 Tevîsatisahassâni nâriyo samalaṅkatâ
Sirinandâ nâma nârî Upaseno nâma atrajo.
23 Nimitte caturo disvâ assayânena nikkhami
anûnanavamâsâni padhânaṃ padahi jino.
24 Brahmunâ yâcito santo Sujâte lokanâyako
vatti cakkaṃ mahavîro Sumaṅgaluyyânamuttame.
25 Sudassano Sudevo ca ahesuṃ aggasâvakâ
Nârado nâm' upaṭṭhâko Sujâtassa mahesino.
26 Nâgâ ca Nâgasamâlâ ca ahesuṃ aggasâvikâ
bodhi tassa bhagavato Mahâveḷûti vuccati.
27 So ca rukkho ghanaruciro acchiddo hoti pattiko
ujuvaṃso brahâ hoti dassaneyyo manoramo.
28 Ekakkhandho pavaḍḍhetvâ tato sâkhâ pabhijjati
yathâ subaddho morahattho evaṃ sobhati so dumo.
29 Na tassa kaṇḍakâ honti nâpi chiddaṃ mahâ ahu
vitthiṇṇasâkho aviralo sannacchâyo manoramo.
30 Sudatto c' eva Citto ca ahesuṃ aggupaṭṭhakâ
Subhaddâ c' eva Padumâ ca ahesuṃ aggupaṭṭhikâ.
31 Paññâsaratano âsi uccatarena so jino
sabbâkâravarûpeto sabbaguṇam upâgato.
32 Tassa pabhâ asamasamâ niddhâvati samantato
appamâṇo atulyo ca opamehi anûpamo.
33 Navutivassasahassâni âyu vijjati tâvade
tâvatâ tiṭṭhamâno so târesi janataṃ bahuṃ.
34 Yathâpi sâgare ummi gagane târakâ yathâ
evaṃ tadâ pâvacanaṃ arahantehi vicitaṃ.

35 So ca buddho asamasamo guṇâni ca tâni atuliyâni
sabbaṃ samantarahitaṃ nanu rittâ sabbasaṅkhârâ.
36 Sujâto jinavaro buddho Silârâmamhi nibbuto
tatth' eva tassa cetiyo tiṇi-gâvutamuggato ti.

SUJÂTASSA BHAGAVATO VAṂSO DVÂDASAMO.

XIV.

PIYADASSI THE THIRTEENTH BUDDHA.

1 Sujâtassa aparena sayambhû lokanâyako
durâsado asamasamo Piyadassî mahâyaso.
2 So pi buddho amitayaso âdicco va virocati
nihantvâna tamaṃ sabbaṃ dhammacakkam pavattayi.
3 Tassâpi atulatejassa ahesuṃ abhisamayâ tayo
Koṭisatasahassânaṃ paṭhamâbhisamayo ahu.
4 Sudassano devarâjâ micchâdiṭṭhiṃ arocayi
tassa diṭṭhiṃ vinodento satthâ dhammam adesayi.
5 Janasannipâto atulo mahâ sannipati tadâ
navutikoṭisahassânaṃ dutiyâbhisamayo ahu.
6 Yadâ doṇamukhaṃ hatthiṃ vinesi narasârathi
asîtikoṭisahassânaṃ tatiyâbhisamayo ahu.
7 Sannipâtâ tayo âsuṃ tassâpi Piyadassino
Koṭisatasahassânaṃ paṭhamo âsi samâgamo.
8 Tato paraṃ navutikoṭî samiṃsu ekato muni
tatiye sannipâtamhi asîtikoṭiyo ahu.
9 Ahaṃ tena samayena Kassapo nâma brâhmaṇo
ajjhâyako mantadharo tiṇṇaṃ vedanâpâragu.
10 Tassa dhammaṃ suṇitvâna pasâdaṃ janayim ahaṃ
koṭisatasahassehi saṅghârâmaṃ amâpayi.
11 Tassa datvâna ârâmaṃ haṭṭho saṃviggamânaso
saraṇaṃ pañcasîlañ ca daḷhaṃ katvâ samâdiyiṃ.
12 So pi maṃ buddho vyâkâsi saṅghamajjhe nisîdiya
Aṭṭharase kappasate ayaṃ buddho bhavissati.

13 Padhânam padahitvâna . . . pe . . . [iv. 13]
. . . pe . . . hessâma sammukhâ imaṃ.
14 Tassâ pi vacanaṃ sutvâ bhîyyo cittam pasâdayi
uttarivatam adhiṭṭhâsiṃ dasapâramipûriyâ.
15 Sudhaññaṃ nâma nagaraṃ Sudatto nâma khattiyo
Sucando nâma janikâ Piyadassissa satthuno.
16 Navavassasahassâni agâraṃ ajjha so vasi
Sunimala-Vimala-Giriguhâ tayo pâsâdamuttamâ.
17 Tettiṃsasatisahassâni nâriyo samalaṅkatâ
Vimalâ nâma nârî ca Kañcanaveḷo nâma atrajo.
18 Nimitte caturo disvâ rathayânena nikkhami
chamâsaṃ padhânacâraṃ acari purisuttamo.
19 Brahmunâ yâcito santo Piyadassî mahâmuni
vatti cakkaṃ mahâvîro Ussâvanuyyâne manorame.
20 Pâlito Sabbadassî ca ahesuṃ aggasâvakâ
Sobhito nâm' upaṭṭhâko Piyadassissa satthuno.
21 Sujâtâ Dhammadinnâ ca ahesuṃ aggasâvikâ
bodhi tassa bhagavato Kakuddho ti pavuccati.
22 Sannako Dhammiko c' eva ahesuṃ aggupaṭṭhakâ
Visâkhâ Dhammadinnâ ca ahesuṃ aggupaṭṭhikâ.
23 So pi buddho amitayaso battiṃsavaralakkhaṇo
asîtihatthamubbedho Sâlarâjâ va dissati.
24 Aggicanda sûriyânaṃ n' atthi tâ disikâ pabhâ
yathâ ahu pabhâ tassa asamassa mahesino.
25 Tassâpi devadevassa âyu tâvatakâ ahu
navutivassasahassâni loke aṭṭhâsi cakkhumâ.
26 So pi buddho asamasamo yugâni pi tâni atuliyâni
sabbaṃ samantarahitaṃ nanu rittâ sabbasaṅkhârâ ti.
27 So Piyadassî muni-varo Asatthârâmamhi nibbuto
tatth' eva tassa jinathûpo tîṇiyojanamuggato ti.

PIYADASSISSA BHAGAVATO VAṂSO TERASAMO.

XV.

ATTHADASSI THE FOURTEENTH BUDDHA.

1 Tatth' eva Maṇḍakappamhi Atthadassî narâsabho
mahâtamaṃ nihantvâna patto sambodhim uttamaṃ.
2 Brahmunâ yâcito santo dhammacakkam pavattayi
amatena tappayi lokaṃ dasasahassî sadevakaṃ.
3 Tassâ pi lokanâthassa ahesuṃ abhisamayâ tayo
koṭisatasahassânaṃ paṭhamâbhisamayo ahu.
4 Yadâ buddho Atthadassî carati devacârikaṃ
koṭisatasahassânaṃ dutiyâbhisamayo ahu.
5 Punâparaṃ yadâ buddho desesi pitu santike
koṭisatasahassânaṃ tatiyâbhisamayo ahu.
6 Sannipâtâ tayo âsuṃ tassâpi ca mahesino.
khîṇâsavânaṃ vimalânaṃ santacittânaṃ tâdinaṃ
7 Aṭṭhanavutisahassânaṃ paṭhamo âsi samâgamo
aṭṭhâsîtisahassânaṃ dutiyo âsi samâgamo.
8 Aṭṭhatiṃsasahassânaṃ tatiyo âsi samâgamo
anupâdânaṃ vimuttânaṃ vimalânaṃ mahesinaṃ
9 Ahaṃ tena samayena jaṭilo uggatâpano
Susimo nâma nâmena mahiyâ seṭṭhasammato.
10 Dibbaṃ mandâravaṃ pupphaṃ padumaṃ pârichattakaṃ
devalokâ pariharitvâ sambuddhaṃ abhipûjayiṃ.
11 So pi maṃ buddho vyâkâsi Atthadassî mahâmuni
aṭṭharase kappasate ayaṃ buddho bhavissati.
12 Padhânaṃ padahitvâna . . . pe . . . [iv. 13]
. . . pe . . . hessâma sammukhâ imaṃ.
13 Tassâpi vacanaṃ sutvâ haṭṭho saṃviggamânaso
uttarivataṃ addhiṭṭhâsiṃ dasapâramipûrayâ.
14 Sobhaṇaṃ nâma nagaraṃ Sâgaro nâma khattiyo
Sudassanâ nâma janikâ Atthadassissa satthuno.
15 Dasavassasahassâni agâraṃ ajjha so vasi
Amaragiri Suragiri Girivâhanâ tayo pâsâdamuttamâ.
16 Tettiṃsañ ca sahassâni nâriyo samalaṅkatâ
Visâkhâ nâma sâ nârî Seno nâm' âsi atrajo.

17 Nimitte caturo disvâ assayânena nikkhami
anûna-aṭṭhamâsâni padhânaṃ padahî jino.
18 Brahmunâ yâcito santo Atthadassî mahâyaso
vatti cakkaṃ mahâvîro Anomuyyâne narâsabho.
19 Santo ca Upasanto ca ahesuṃ aggasâvakâ
Abhayo nâm' upaṭṭhâko Atthadassissa satthuno.
20 Dhammâ c' eva Sudhammâ ca ahesum aggasâvikâ
bodhi tassa bhagavato Campako ti pavuccati.
21 Nakulo ca Nisabho ca ahesum aggupaṭṭhakâ
Makilâ ca Sunandâ ca ahesum aggupaṭṭhikâ.
22 So pi buddho asamasamo asîtihatthamuggato
sobhati Sâlarâjâ va Uḷurâjâ va pûrito.
23 Tassa pâkaṭikâ ramsî anekasatakoṭiyo
uddham adho dasadisâ pharanti yojanaṃ tadâ.
24 So pi buddho narâsabho sabbasattuttamo muni
vassasatasahassâni loke aṭṭhâsi cakkhumâ.
25 Atulaṃ datvâna obhâsaṃ virocetvâ sadevake
so pi aniccataṃ patto yath' aggupâdânasaṅkhayâ.
26 Atthadassî jinavaro Anomârâmamhi nibbuto
dhâtuvitthârikam âsi tesu tesu padesato ti.

ATTHADASSISSA BHAGAVATO VAMSO CUDDASAMO.

XVI.

DHAMMADASSI THE FIFTEENTH BUDDHA.

1 Tatth' eva Maṇḍakappamhi Dhammadassî mahâyaso
tam andhakâraṃ vidhametvâ atirocati sadevake.
2 Tassâpi atulatejassa dhammacakkappavattane
koṭisatasahassânaṃ paṭhamâbhisamayo ahu.
3 Yadâ buddho Dhammadassî vinesi Sañjayam isiṃ
tadâ navutikoṭînaṃ dutiyâbhisamayo ahu.
4 Yadâ Sakko upâgañchi sapariso vinâyakaṃ
tadâ asîtikoṭînaṃ tatiyâbhisamayo ahu.
5 Tassâ pi devadevassa sannipâtâ tayo ahuṃ
khîṇâsavânaṃ vimalânaṃ santacittânaṃ tâdinaṃ.
6 Yadâ buddho Dhammadassî saraṇe vassaṃ upâgami
tadâ koṭisahassânaṃ paṭhamo âsi samâgamo.
7 Punâparaṃ yadâ buddho devato ehi mânuse
tadâpi satakotînaṃ dutiyo âsi samâgamo.
8 Punâparaṃ yadâ buddho pakâsesi dhûte guṇe
tadâ asîtikoṭînaṃ tatiyo âsi samâgamo.
9 Ahaṃ tena samayena Sakko âsiṃ purindado
dibbagandhena mâlena turiyena abhipûjayiṃ.
10 So pi maṃ buddho vyâkâsi devamajjhe nisîdiya
aṭṭharase kappasate ayaṃ buddho bhavissati.
11 Padhânaṃ padahitvâna . . . pe . . . [iv. 13]
. . . pe . . . hessâma sammukhâ imaṃ.
12 Tassâpi vacanaṃ sutvâ bhîyyo cittaṃ pasâdayiṃ
uttarivataṃ adhiṭṭhâsiṃ dasapâramipûriyâ.
13 Saraṇaṃ nâma nagaraṃ Saraṇo nàma khattiyo
Sunandâ nâma janikâ Dhammadassissa satthuno.
14 Aṭṭhavassasahassâni agâraṃ ajjha so vasi
Arajo Virajo Sudassano tayo pâsâdamuttamâ.
15 Ticattârîsahassâni nâriyo samalaṅkatâ
Vicitoḷî nâma nârî atrajo Puññavaḍḍhano.

16 Nimitte caturo disvâ pâsâdenâbhinikkhami
sattâhaṃ padhânacâraṃ acari purisuttamo.
17 Brahmunâ yâcito santo Dhammadassî narâsabho
vatti cakkaṃ mahavîro Migadâye naruttamo.
18 Padumo Phussadevo ca ahesum aggasâvakâ
Sunetto nâm' upaṭṭhâko Dhamadassissa satthuno.
19 Khemâ ca Saccanâmâ ca ahesum aggasâvikâ
bodhi tassa bhagavato Bimbajâlo ti vuccati.
20 Subhaddo Kaṭisaho c' eva ahesum aggupaṭṭhakâ
Sâḷiyâ ca Vaḷiyâ ca ahesum aggupaṭṭhikâ.
21 So pi buddho asamasamo asîtihatthamuggato
atirocati tejena dasasahassambhi dhâtuyâ.
22 Suphullo Sâlarâjâ va vijju va gagane yathâ
majjhantike va suriyo evaṃ so upasobhittha.
23 Tassâpi atulatejassa samakaṃ âsi jîvitaṃ
vassasatasahassâni loke aṭṭhâsi cakkhumâ.
24 Obhâsaṃ dassayitvâna vimalaṃ katvâna sâsanaṃ
virocayi cando va gagane nibbuto so sasâvako.
25 Dhammadassî mahavîro Kesârâmamhi nibbuto
tatth' eva so thûpavaro tiyojanasamuggato ti.

DHAMMADASSISSA BHAGAVATO VAṂSO PANNARASAMO.

XVII.

SIDDHATTHA THE SIXTEENTH BUDDHA.

1 Dhammadassissa aparena Siddhattho nâma nâyako
'nîharitvâ tamaṃ sabbaṃ suriyo abbhuggato yathâ.
2 So pi patvâna sambodhiṃ santârento sadevakaṃ
abhivassi dhammameghena nibbâpento sadevakaṃ.
3 Tassâ pi atulatejassa ahesuṃ abhisamayâ tayo
koṭisatasahassânaṃ paṭhamâbhisamayo ahu.
4 Punâparaṃ bhîmaraṭṭhe yadi âhani duddrabhiṃ
tadâ navutikoṭînaṃ dutiyâbhisamayo ahu.
5 Yadâ buddho dhammaṃ desesi Vebhâre so puruttame
tâdâ navutikoṭînaṃ tatiyâbhisamayo ahu.
6 Sannipâtâ tayo âsuṃ tasmim pi dîpaduttame
khîṇâsavânaṃ vimalânaṃ santacittânaṃ tâdinaṃ.
7 Koṭisatânaṃ navutînam asîtiyâ ca koṭînaṃ
Ete âsuṃ tayo ṭhânâ vimalânaṃ samâgame.
8 Ahaṃ tena samayena Maṅgalo nâma tâpaso
uggatejo duppasaho abhiññâbalasamâhito.
9 Jambuto phalam âhatvâ Siddhatthasso adâs' ahaṃ
paṭiggahetvâ sambuddho idaṃ vacanam abravi :—
10 Passattha imaṃ tâpasaṃ jaṭilaṃ uggatâpanaṃ
catunavute ito kappe ayaṃ buddho bhavissati.
11 Padhânaṃ padahitvâna . . . pe . . . [iv. 13]
. . . pe . . . hessâma sammukhâ imaṃ.
12 Tassâ pi vacanaṃ sutvâ bhîyyo cittaṃ pasâdayi
uttari vatam adhiṭṭhâsiṃ dasapâramipûriyâ.
13 Vebhâraṃ nâma nagaraṃ Udeno nâma khattiyo
Suphassâ nâma janikâ Siddatthassa mahesino.
14 Dasavassasahassâni agaraṃ ajjha so vasi
Kokâs'-uppala-kokanudâ tayo pâsâdamuttamâ.
15 Tissoḷassa sahassâni nâriyo samalaṅkatâ
Sumanâ nâma sâ nârî Anupamo nâma atrajo.
16 Nimitte caturo disvâ savikâyânena nikkhami
anûnadasamâsâni paddhânaṃ padahi jino.

17 Brahmunâ yâcito santo Siddhattho lokanâyako
vatti cakkaṃ mahâvîro Migadâye naruttamo.
18 Samphalo ca Sumitto ca ahesuṃ aggasâvakâ
Revato nâma upaṭṭhâko Siddhatthassa mahesino.
19 Sîvalâ ca Surâmâ ca ahesuṃ aggasâvikâ
bodhi tassa bhagavato Kaṇikâro ti vuccati.
20 Suppiyo ca Samuddo ca ahesuṃ aggupaṭṭhakâ
Rammâ c' eva Surammâ ca ahesuṃ aggupaṭṭhikâ.
21 So buddho saṭṭhiratanaṃ ahosi nabhamuggato
kañcanagghikasaṅkâso dasahassî virocati.
22 So pi buddho asamasamo atulo appaṭipuggalo
vassasatasahassâni loke atthâsi cakkhumâ.
23 Vimalaṃ pabhaṃ dassayitvâ pupphâpetvânâ sâvake
vilâsetvâ ca samâpattiyâ nibbuto so sasâvako.
24 Siddhattho muni varo buddho Anomârâmamhi nibbuto
tatth' eva so thûpavaro catuyojanamuggato ti.

SIDDHATTHASSA BHAGAVATO VAṂSO SOḶASAMO.

XVIII.

TISSA THE SEVENTEENTH BUDDHA.

1 Siddhatthassa aparena asamo appaṭipuggalo
anantasîlo amitayaso Tisso lokagganâyako.
2 Tam andhakâraṃ vidhamitvâ obhâsetvâ sadevakaṃ
anukampako mahavîro loke uppajji cakkhumâ.
3 Tassâpi atulâ iddhi atulasîlasamadhî ca
sabbattha pâramiṃ gantvâ dhamma cakkaṃ pavattayi.
4 So buddho dasasahassamhi viññâpesi giraṃ suciṃ
koṭisatasahassâni samiṃsu paṭhame dhammadesane
5 Dutiye navutikoṭînaṃ tatiye saṭṭhi koṭiyo.
bandhanâ so vimocesi sampatte naramarû tadâ.
6 Sannipâtâ tayo âsuṃ Tisse lokagganâyake
khîṇâsavânaṃ vimalânaṃ santacittânaṃ tâdinaṃ.
7 Khîṇâsavasahassânaṃ paṭhamo âsi samâgamo.
navutisatasahassânaṃ dutiyo âsi samâgamo.

8 Asîtisatasahassânaṃ tatiyo âsi samâgamo.
khîṇâsavânaṃ vimalânaṃ pupphitânaṃ vimuttiyâ.
9 Ahaṃ tena samayena Sujâto nâma khattiyo
mahâbhogaṃ chaḍḍayitvâ pabbajiṃ isi-pabbajjaṃ.
10 Mayi pabbajite sante uppajji lokanâyako
buddho ti saddaṃ sutvâna pîti me upapajjatha.
11 Dibbaṃ mandâravaṃ pupphaṃ padumaṃ pârichattakaṃ
ubho hatthehi paggayha dhunamâno upâgamiṃ.
12 Catuvaṇṇaparivutaṃ Tissaṃ lokagganâyakaṃ
tam ahaṃ pupphaṃ gahetvâna matthake dhârayiṃ jinaṃ.
13 So pi maṃ buddho vyâkâsi janamajjhe nisîdiya
dve navute ito kappe ayaṃ buddho bhavissati.
14 Padhânaṃ padahitvâna . . . pe . . . [iv. 13]
. . . pe . . . hessâma sammûkhâ imaṃ.
15 Tassâpi vacanaṃ sutvâ bhîyyo cittaṃ pasâdayi
uttarivataṃ adhiṭṭhâsiṃ dasapâramipûriyâ.
16 Khemakaṃ nâma nagaraṃ Janasandho nâma khattiyo
Padumâ nâma janikâ Tissassa ca mahesino.
17 Sattavassasahassâni agâraṃ ajjha so vasi
Guhâsela-nârî-nisabhâ tayo pâsâdamuttamâ.
18 Samatiṃsasahassâni nâriyo samalaṅkatâ
Subhaddâ nâma sâ nârî Ânando nâma atrajo.
19 Nimitte caturo disvâ assayânena nikkhami
anûnakaṃ aṭṭhamâsam padhânaṃ padahi jino.
20 Brahmunâ yâcito santo Tisso lokagganâyako
vatti cakkaṃ mahavîro Yasavatiyam uttame.
21 Brahmadevo Udayo ca ahesuṃ aggasâvakâ
Samaṅgo nâm' upaṭṭhâko Tissassa ca mahesino.
22 Phussâ c' eva Sudattâ ca ahesuṃ aggasâvikâ
bodhi tassa bhagavato Asano ti pavuccati.
23 Sambalo ca Siri c' eva ahesum aggupaṭṭhakâ
Kissâgotamî Upasenâ ahesum aggupaṭṭhikâ.
24 So pi buddho saṭṭhiratano âhu uccatarena jino
anupamo asadiso Himavâ viya dissati.
25 Tassâpi atulatejassa âyu âsi anuttaro
vassasatasahassâni loke aṭṭhâsi cakkhumâ.
26 Uttamam pavaraṃ seṭṭham anubhotvâ mahâyasaṃ
jalitvâ aggikkhandho va nibbuto so sasâvako.

27 Valâhako va anilena suriyena viya ussavo
andhakâro va dîpena nibbuto so sasâvako.
28 Tisso jinavaro buddho Nandârâmamhi nibbuto
tatth' eva tassa jinathûpo tîṇiyojanamussito ti.

TISSASSA BHAGAVATO VAṂSO SATTARASAMO.

XIX.

PHUSSA THE EIGHTEENTH BUDDHA.

1 Tatth' eva Maṇḍakappamhi âhu satthâ anuttaro
anupamo asamasamo Phusso lokagganâyako.
2 So pi sabbaṃ tamaṃ hatvâ vijaṭetvâ mahâjaṭaṃ
sadevakaṃ tappayanto abhivassi amatambuyâ.
3 Dhammacakkappavattente Phusse nakkhattamaṅgale
koṭisatasahassânaṃ paṭhamâbhisamayo ahu
4 Navutisatasahassânaṃ dutiyâbhisamayo ahu
asîtisatasahassânaṃ tatiyâbhisamayo ahu.
5 Sannipâtâ tayo âsuṃ Phussassa pi mahesino
khîṇâsavânaṃ vimalânaṃ santacittânaṃ tâdinaṃ.
6 Saṭṭhisatasahassânaṃ paṭhamo âsi samâgamo
paññâsasatasahassânaṃ dutiyo âsi samâgamo
7 Cattârimsaṃ satasahassânaṃ tatiyo âsi samâgamo
anupâdâvimuttânaṃ vocchinnaṃ paṭisandhinaṃ.
8 Ahaṃ tena samayena Vijitavî nâma khattiyo
chaḍḍayitvâna mahârajjaṃ pabbajiṃ tassa santike.
9 So pi maṃ buddho vyâkâsi Phusso lokagganâyako
ito dve navute kappe ayaṃ buddho bhavissati.
10 Padhânam padahitvâna . . . pe . . . [iv. 13]
. . . pe . . . hessâma sammukhâ imaṃ.
11 Tassâpi vacanaṃ sutvâ bhîyyo cittam pasâdayi
uttarivataṃ adhiṭṭhâsiṃ dasamapâramipûriyâ.
12 Suttantaṃ vinayaṃ câpi navaṅgaṃ satthu sâsanaṃ
sabbaṃ pariyâpuṇitvâna sobhayiṃ jinasâsanaṃ.

13 Tatth' appamatto viharanto brahmaṃ bhâvetvâ bhâvanaṃ
abhiññâsu pâramiṃ gantvâ brahmalokam agacch' aham.
14 Kâsikaṃ nâma nagaraṃ Jayaseno nâma khattiyo
Sirimâ nâma janikâ Phussassa pi mahesino.
15 Chabbassasahassânaṃ agâraṃ ajjha so vasi
Garuḷa-Haṃsa-Suvaṇṇabharâ tayo pâsâdamuttamâ.
16 Tevîsatisahassâni nâriyo samalaṅkatâ
Kisâgotamî nâma nârî Ânando nâma atrajo.
17 Nimitte caturo disvâ hatthiyânena nikkhami
Chamâsaṃ padhânaṃ câraṃ acari purisuttamo.
18 Brahmunâ yâcito santo Phusso lokagganâyako
vatti cakkaṃ mahâvîro Migadâye naruttamo.
19 Sukhito Dhammaseno ca ahesuṃ aggasâvakâ
Sambhiyo nâm' upaṭṭhâko Phussassa ca mahesino.
20 Câlâ ca Upacâlâ ca ahesuṃ aggasâvikâ
bodhi tassa bhagavato Âmaṇḍo ti pavuccati.
21 Dhanañjayo Visâkho ca ahesuṃ aggupaṭṭhakâ
Padumâ c' eva Nâgâ ca ahesuṃ aggupaṭṭhikâ.
22 Aṭṭhapaññâsaratanaṃ so pi accugato muni
sobhati sataraṃsi va uḷurâjâ va pûrito.
23 Navutivassasahassâni âyu vijjati tâvade
tâvatâ tiṭṭhamâno so târesi janataṃ bahuṃ.
24 Ovâdetvâ bahû satte santâretvâ mahâjane
So pi satthâ atulayaso nibbuto so sasâvako.
25 Phusso jinavaro satthâ Sonârâmamhi nibbuto
dhâtuvitthârikam âsi tesu tesu padesato ti.

PHUSASSA BHAGAVATO VAṂSO AṬṬHÂRASAMO.

XX.

VIPASSI THE NINETEENTH BUDDHA.

1 Phussassa ca aparena sambuddho dvipaduttamo.
Vipassî nâma nâmena loke uppajji cakkhumâ.
2 Avijjaṃ sabbam padâletvâ patto sambodhim uttamaṃ
dhammacakkaṃ pavattetum pakkâmi Bandhumatim puraṃ.
3 Dhammacakkam pavattetvâ ubho bodhesi nâyako
gaṇanâya na vattabo paṭhamâbhisamayo ahu.
4 Punâparam amitayaso tattha saccaṃ pakâsayi
caturâsîtisahassânaṃ dutiyâbhisamayo ahu.
5 Caturâsîtisahassâni sambuddham anupabbajuṃ
tesaṃ ârâmapattânaṃ dhammaṃ desesi cakkhumâ.
6 Sabbâkârena bhâsato sutvâ upanisâ jino
te pi dhammaṃ varaṃ gantvâ tatiyâbhisamayo ahu.
7 Sannipâtâ tayo âsuṃ Vipassissa mahesino
khîṇâsavânaṃ vimalânaṃ santacittânaṃ tâdinaṃ.
8 Aṭṭhasaṭṭhisahassânaṃ paṭhamo âsi samâgamo
bhikkusatasahassânaṃ dutiyo âsi samâgamo.
9 Asîtibhikkhusahassânaṃ tatiyo âsi samâgamo.
Tattha bhikkhugaṇamajjhe sambuddho atirocati.
10 Ahaṃ tena samayena Nâgarâjâ mahiddhiko
Atulo nâma nâmena puññavanto jutindharo.
11 Nekânaṃ nâgakoṭînam parivâretvâu' ahaṃ tadâ
vajjanto dibbaturiyehi lokajeṭṭhaṃ upâgamiṃ.
12 Upasaṅkamitvâ sambuddhaṃ Vipassiṃ lokanâyakaṃ
maṇimuttaratanakhacitaṃ sabbâbharaṇabhûsitaṃ
Nimantetvâ dhammarâjassa suvaṇṇam piṭṭham adâs' ahaṃ.
13 So pi maṃ buddho vyâkâsi saṅghamajjhe nisîdiya
ito ekanavute kappe ayaṃ buddho bhavissati.
14 Ahu Kapilavhaye ramme nikkhamitvâ Tathâgato
padhânaṃ padahitvâna katvâ dukkarakâriyaṃ.

15 Ajapâlarukkhamûlamhi nisîditvâ Tathâgato
tattha pâyâsam paggayha Nerañjaram upehiti.
16 Nerañjarâya tîramhi pâyâsam asati jino
paṭiyattavaramaggena bodhimûlam upehiti.
17 Tato padakkhiṇaṃ katvâ bodhimaṇḍam anuttaraṃ
Assatthamûle sambodhiṃ bujjhissati mahâyaso.
18 Imassa janikâ mâtâ Mâyâ nâma bhavissati
pitâ Suddhodano nâma ayaṃ hessati Gotamo.
19 Anâsavâ vîtarâgâ santacittâ samâhitâ
Kolito Upatisso ca aggâ hessanti sâvakâ.
20 Ânando nam' upaṭṭhâko upaṭṭhissati maṃ jinaṃ
Khemâ Uppalavaṇṇâ ca aggâ hessanti sâvikâ
21 Anâsavâ vîtarâgâ santacittâ samâhitâ.
bodhi tassa bhagavato Assattho ti pavuccati.
22 Tassâhaṃ vacanaṃ sutvâ bhîyyo cittam pasâdayiṃ
uttarivatam adhiṭṭhâsiṃ dasapâramipûriyâ.
23 Nagaraṃ Bandhumatî nâma Bandhumo nâma khattiyo
mâtâ Bandhumatî nâma Vipassissa mahesino.
24 Aṭṭhavassasahassâni agâram ajjha so vasi.
Nando Sunando Sirimâ tayo pâsâdamuttamâ.
25 Ticattâri sahassâni nâriyo samalaṅkatâ.
Sutanâ nâma sâ nârî Saṃvaṭṭakkhaṇdo nâm' atrajo.
26 Nimitte caturo disvâ rathayânena nikkhami
anûnaaṭṭhamâsâni padhânaṃ padahi jino.
27 Brahmunâ yâcito santo Vipassî lokanâyako
vatti cakkaṃ mahavîro Migadâye naruttamo.
28 Khandho ca Tisso nâma ca ahesuṃ aggasâvakâ
Asoko nâm' upaṭṭhâko Vipassissa mahesino.
29 Candâ ca Candamittâ ca ahesum aggasâvikâ:
bodhi tassa bhagavato Pâṭalî ti pavuccati.
30 Punabbasumitto Nâgo ca ahesum aggupaṭṭhakâ
Sirimâ Uttarâ c' eva ahesum aggupaṭṭhikâ.
31 Asîtihatthamubbedho Vipassî lokanâyako
pabhâ niddhâvati tassa samantâ sattayojane.
32 Asîtivassasahassâni âyu buddhassa tâvade
tâvatâ tiṭṭhamâno so târesi janataṃ bahuṃ.
33 Bahudevamanussânaṃ bandhanam parimocayi
maggâmaggañ ca âcikkhi avasesaputhujjane.

34 Âlokaṃ dassayitvâna desitvâ amatam padaṃ
jalitvâ aggikkhandho va nibbuto so sasâvako.
35 Iddhivaram puññavaraṃ lakkhaṇañ catubhûmikaṃ.
sabbaṃ samantarahitaṃ nanu rittâ sabbasaṅkhârâ.
36 Vipassî jinavaro dhîro Sumittârâmamhi nibbuto.
tatth' eva tassa thûpavaro sattayojanamussito ti.

VIPASSISSA BHAGAVATO VAṂSO EKÛNAVÎSATIMO.

XXI.

SIKHI THE TWENTIETH BUDDHA.

1 Vipassissa aparena sambuddho dvipaduttamo
Sikhisavhayo nâma jino asamo appaṭipuggalo.
2 Marasenaṃ pamadditvâ patto sambodhim uttamaṃ
dhammacakkaṃ pavattesi anukampâya pâṇinaṃ.
3 Dhammacakkappavattente Sikhimhi jinapuṅgave
koṭisatasahassânaṃ paṭhamâbhisamayo ahu.
4 Aparam pi dhammaṃ desente gaṇaseṭṭhe naruttame
navutikoṭisahassânaṃ dutiyâbhisamayo ahu.
5 Yamakam pâṭihîrañ ca dassayante sadevake
asîtikoṭisahassânaṃ tatiyâbhisamayo ahu.
6 Sannipâtâ tayo âsuṃ Sikhissâpi mahesino
khîṇâsavânaṃ vimalânaṃ santacittânaṃ tâdinaṃ.
7 Bhikkhusatasahassânaṃ paṭhamo âsi samâgamo.
asîtibhikkhusahassânaṃ dutiyo âsi samâgamo
8 Sattatibhikkhusahassânaṃ tatiyo âsi samâgamo.
anupalitto padumaṃ va toyamhi sampavaḍḍhitaṃ.
9 Ahaṃ tena samayena Arindamo nâma khattiyo
sambuddhapamukhaṃ saṅghaṃ annapânena tappayiṃ.
10 Bahuṃ dussavaraṃ datvâ dussakoṭim anappakaṃ
alaṅkataṃ hatthiyânaṃ sambuddhassa adâs' ahaṃ.
11 Hatthiyânaṃ nimminitvâ kappiyaṃ upanâmayiṃ
pûrayiṃ mânasaṃ mayhaṃ niccaṃ daḷham upaṭṭhitaṃ.

12 So pi maṃ buddho vyâkâsi Sikhî lokagganâyako
ekatiṃse ito kappe ayaṃ buddho bhavissati.
13 Ahu Kapilavhaye ramme . . . pe . . . [xx. 14]
. . . pe . . . hessâma sammukhâ imaṃ. [iv. 13]
14 Tassâhaṃ vacanaṃ sutvâ bhîyyo cittam pasâdayiṃ
uttarivatam adhiṭṭhâsiṃ dasapâramipûriyâ.
15 Nagaraṃ Aruṇavatî nâma Aruṇo nâma Khattiyo
Pabhâvatî nâma janikâ Sikhissa ca mahesino.
16 Sattavassasahassâni agâram ajjha so vasi
Sucando Giri Vahano tayo pâsâdamuttamâ.
17 Catuvîsatisahassâni nâriyo samalaṅkatâ
Sabbakâmâ nâma nârî Atulo nâma atrajo.
18 Nimitte caturo disvâ hatthiyânena nikkhami
aṭṭhamâsaṃ padhânacâraṃ acari purisuttamo.
19 Brahmunâ yâcito santo Sikhî lokagganâyako
Vatti cakkaṃ mahâvîro Migadâye naruttamo.
20 Abhibhû Sambhavo nâma ahesum aggasâvakâ
Khemaṅkaro upaṭṭhâko Sikhissa pi mahesino.
21 Akhilâ c' eva Padumâ ca ahesum aggasâvikâ
bodhi tassa bhagavato Puṇḍarîko ti vuccati.
22 Sirivaḍḍho ca Cando ca ahesum aggupaṭṭhakâ
Cittâ c' eva Suguttâ ca ahesum aggupaṭṭhikâ.
23 Uccatarena so buddho sattatihatthamuggato
Kañcanagghikasaṇkâso dvattiṃsavaralakkhaṇo.
24 Tassâpi byâmappabhâ kâyâ divâ rattiṃ nirantaraṃ
disodisaṃ niccharanti tîṇiyojanaso pabhâ.
25 Sattativassasahassâni âyu tassa mahesino
tâvatâ tiṭṭhamâno so târesi janataṃ bahuṃ.
26 Dhammamegho pavassetvâ temayitvâ sadevake
kheman taṃ pâpayitvâna nibbuto so sasâvako.
27 Anuvyañjanâsampannaṃ dvattiṃsavaralakkhaṇaṃ
sabbaṃ samantarahitaṃ nanu rittâ sabbasaṅkhârâ.
28 Sikhî munivaro buddho Dussârâmamhi nibbuto
tatth' eva tassa thûpavaro tîṇiyojanamuggato ti.

SIKHISSA BHAGAVATO VAṂSO VÎSATIMO.

XXII.

VESSABHU THE TWENTY-FIRST BUDDHA.

1 Tatth' eva Maṇḍakappamhi asamo appaṭipuggalo
Vessabhû nâma nâmena loke uppajji so jino.
2 Âdittaṃ ti ca râgaggitaṇhânaṃ vijitaṃ sadâ
nâgo va bandhanaṃ chetvâ patto sambodhim uttamaṃ.
3 Dhammacakkappavattente Vesabhû lokanâyako
asîtikoṭisahassânaṃ paṭhamâbhisamayo ahu.
4 Pakkante cârikaṃ raṭṭhe lokajeṭṭhe narâsabhe
sattatikoṭisahassânaṃ dutiyâbhisamayo ahu.
5 Mahâdiṭṭhiṃ vinodento pâṭihîraṃ karoti so
samâgatâ naramarû dasasahassî sadevake.
6 Mahâ-acchariyaṃ disvâ abbhutaṃ lomahaṃsanaṃ
devâ c' eva manussâ ca bujjhare saṭṭhikoṭiyo.
7 Sannipâtâ tayo âsuṃ Vessabhussa mahesino
khîṇâsavânaṃ vimalânaṃ santacittânaṃ tâdinaṃ.
8 Asîtibhikkhusahassânaṃ paṭhamo âsi samâgamo
sattatibhikkhusahassânaṃ dutiyo âsi samâgamo
9 Saṭṭhibhikkhusahassânaṃ tatiyo âsi samâgamo
jarâdibhayacittânaṃ orasânaṃ mahesinaṃ.
10 Tassa buddhassa asamassa cakkaṃ vattayim uttamaṃ
sutvâna panîtaṃ dhammam pabbajjam abhirocayi.
11 Ahaṃ tena samayena Sudassano nâma khattiyo
annapânena vatthena sasaṅghaṃ jinam pûjayiṃ.
12 Mahâdânam pavattetvâ rattiṃ divam atandito
pabbajjaṃ guṇasampannaṃ pabbajiṃ jinasantike.
13 Âcâraguṇasampanno vattasîlasamâhito
sabbaññutaṃ gavesanto ramâmi jinasâsane.
14 Saddhâ pîti upagantvâ buddhaṃ vandâmi sattharaṃ
pîti uppajjati mayhaṃ bodhiyâ yeva kâraṇâ.
15 Anivattamânasaṃ ñatvâ sambuddho etad abrâvi :—
ekatiṃse ito kappe ayaṃ buddho bhavissati.
16 Ahu Kapilavahye ramme . . . pe . . . [xx. 14]
. . . pe . . . hessâma sammukhâ imaṃ. [iv. 13]

17 Tassâhaṃ vacanaṃ sutvâ bhîyyo cittam pasâdayiṃ
uttarivatam adhiṭṭhâsiṃ dasapâramipûriyâ.
18 Anomaṃ nâma nagaraṃ Supatito nâma khattiyo
mâtâ Yasavatî nâma Vessabhussa mahesino.
19 Chabbassasahassânam agâram ajjha so vasi
Ruci-Suruci-Vaḍḍhanâ tayo pâsâdamuttamâ.
20 Anûnatiṃsasahassâni nâriyo samalaṅkatâ
Sucittâ nâma sâ nârî Supabuddho nâma atrajo.
21 Nimitte caturo disvâ sivikâyânâbhinikkhami
chamâsam padhânacâram acari purisuttamo.
22 Brahmunâ yâcito santo Vessabhû lokaṇâyako
vatti cakkaṃ mahâvîro Aruṇârâme naruttame.
23 Soṇo ca Uttaro c' eva ahesum aggasâvakâ
Upasanto nâm' upaṭṭhâko Vessabhussa mahesino.
24 Dâmâ c' eva Samâlâ ca ahesum aggasâvikâ
bodhi tassa bhagavato Mahâsâlo ti vuccati.
25 Soṭṭhiko c' eva Rammo ca ahesuṃ aggupaṭṭhakâ
Gotamî ca Sirimâ ca ahesuṃ aggupaṭṭhikâ.
26 Saṭṭhiratanam-ubbedho Hemayûpasamupamo
kâyâ niccharati raṃsi ratti va pabbate Sikhî.
27 Saṭṭhivassasahassâni âyu vijjati tâvade
tâvatâ tiṭṭhamâno so târesi janataṃ bahuṃ.
28 Dhammaṃ vitthârikaṃ katvâ vibhajitvâ mahâjanaṃ
dhammanâvaṃ ṭhapetvâna nibbuto so sasâvako.
29 Dassaneyyaṃ mahâjanaṃ vihâraṃ c' iriyâpathaṃ
sabbaṃ samantarahitaṃ nanu rittâ sabbasaṅkhârâ.
30 Vessabhû jinavaro satthâ Khemârâmhi nibbuto
dhâtuvitthârikam âsi tesu tesu padesato ti.

VESSABHUSSA BHAGAVATO VAṂSO EKAVÎSATIMO.

XXIII.

KAKUSANDHA THE TWENTY-SECOND BUDDHA.

1 Vessabhussa aparena sambuddho dvipaduttamo
Kakusandho nâma nâmena appameyyo durâsado.
2 Ugghâṭetvâ sabbabhavaṃ cariyâ-pâramiṅgato
Sîho va pañjaraṃ bhetvâ patto sambodhim uttamaṃ.
3 Dhammacakkappavattente Kakusandhe lokanâyake
cattârîsaṃ koṭisahassânaṃ paṭhamâbhisamayo ahu.
4 Antalikkhamhi âkâse yamakam katvâ vikubbanaṃ
tiṃsakoṭisahassânaṃ bodhesi devamânuse.
5 Naradevassa yakkhassa catusaccappakâsane
dhammâbhisamayo tassa gaṇanâto asaṅkheyyo.
6 Kakusandhassa bhagavato eko âsi samâgamo
khîṇâsavânaṃ vimalânaṃ santacittânaṃ tâdinaṃ.
7 Cattâlîsasahassânaṃ tadâ âsi samâgamo
dantabhûmim anuppattânaṃ âsavâdi-gaṇakkhayâ.
8 Ahaṃ tena samayena Khemo nâmâsi khattiyo
Tathâgate jinaputte dânaṃ datvâ anappakaṃ.
9 Pattañ ca cîvaraṃ datvâ añjanaṃ madhulaṭṭhikaṃ
ime tam patthitaṃ sabbaṃ paṭiyâdemi varaṃ varaṃ.
10 So pi maṃ muni vyâkâsi Kakusandho vinâyako
imamhi bhaddake kappe ayaṃ buddho bhavissati.
11 Ahu Kapilavhaye ramme . . . pe . . . [xx. 14]
. . . pe . . . hessâma sammukhâ imaṃ. [iv. 13]
12 Tassâhaṃ vacanaṃ sutvâ bhîyyo cittaṃ pasâdayiṃ
uttarivatam adhiṭṭhâsiṃ dasapâramipûriyâ.
13 Nagaraṃ Khemavatî nâma Khemo nâma s' ahaṃ tadâ
sabbaññutaṃ gavesanto pabbajiṃ tassa santike.
14 Brâhmaṇo Aggidatto ca âsi buddhassa so pitâ
Visâkhâ nâma janikâ Kakusandhassa mahesino.
15 Vasi tattha Khemapure sambuddhassa mahâkulaṃ
narânaṃ pavaraṃ seṭṭhaṃ jâtimantaṃ mahâyasaṃ
16 Catuvassasahassâni agâram ajjha so vasi
Ruci-Suruci-Vaḍḍhaṇâ tayo pâsâdamuttamâ.

17 Samatiṃsasahassâni nâriyo samalaṅkatâ
Virocamânâ nâma nârî Uttaro nâma atrajo.
18 Nimitte caturo disvâ rathayânena nikkhami
anûnakaṃ aṭṭhamâsaṃ padhânaṃ padahi jino.
19 Brahmunâ yâcito santo Kakusandho lokanâyako
vatti cakkaṃ mahavîro Migadâye naruttamo.
20 Vidhuro Sañjîvo nâma ca ahesuṃ aggasâvakâ
Buddhijo nâm' uppaṭṭhâko Kakusandhassa satthuno
21 Samâ ca Campanâmâ ca ahesuṃ aggasâvikâ
bodhi tassa bhagavato Sirîso ti pavuccati.
22 Accuto ca Samano ca ahesuṃ aggupaṭṭhakâ
Nandâ c' eva Sunandâ ca ahesuṃ aggupaṭṭhikâ.
23 Cattarârîsaratanâni accugato mahâmuni
Kanakappabhâ niccharanti samantâ dvâdasayojanaṃ.
24 Cattârîsavasasahassâni âyu tassa mahesino
tâvatâ tiṭṭhamâno târesi janataṃ bahuṃ.
25 Dhammâpaṇaṃ pasâretvâ naranârînaṃ sadevake
naditvâ sîhanâdañ ca nibbuto so sasâvako.
26 Aṭṭhaṅgavacanasampanno acchiddâni nirantaraṃ
sabbaṃ samantarahitaṃ nanu rittâ sabbasaṅkhârâ.
27 Kakusandho jinavaro Khemârâmamhi nibbuto
tatth' eva tassa thûpavaro gâvutanabhamuggato ti.

KAKUSANDHASSA BHAGAVATO VAṂSO DVÂVÎSATIMO.

XXIV.

KOṆÂGAMANA THE TWENTY-THIRD BUDDHA.

1 Kakusandhassa aparena Sambuddho dvipaduttamo
Koṇâgamano nâma jino lokajeṭṭho narâsabho.
2 Dasadhamme pûrayitvâna kantâraṃ samatikkami
pavâhiya malaṃ sabbaṃ patto sambodhim uttamaṃ.
3 Dhammacakkappavattente Konâgamane nâyake
tiṃsakoṭisahassânaṃ paṭhamâbhisamayo ahu.
4 Pâṭihîraṃ karonte ca paravâdappamaddane
vîsatikoṭisahassânaṃ dutiyâbhisamayo ahu.
5 Tato vikubbanaṃ katvâ jino devapuraṃ gato
vasati tattha sambuddho silâyaṃ paṇḍukambale.
6 Pakaraṇe satta desento vassaṃ vasati so muni
dasakoṭisahassânaṃ tatiyâbhisamayo ahu.
7 Tassâpi devadevassa eko âsi samâgamo
khîṇâsavânaṃ vimalânaṃ santacittânaṃ tâdinaṃ.
8 Tiṃsabhikkhu sahassânaṃ tadâ âsi samâgamo
atikkanta-catur'-oghânaṃ bhijjitânañ ca maccuyâ.
9 Ahaṃ tena samayena Pabbato nâma khattiyo
mittâmaccehi sampanno anantabalavâhano.
10 Sambuddhadassanaṃ gantvâ sutvâ dhammam anuttaraṃ
nimantetvâ sajinaṃ saṅghaṃ dânaṃ datvâ yathicchakaṃ.
11 Paṭṭunnaṃ cînapaṭṭañ ca koseyyaṃ kambalaṃ pi ca
sovaṇṇapâdukañ c' eva adâsiṃ satthusâvake.
12 So pi maṃ muni vyâkâsi saṅghamajjhe nisîdiya
imasmiṃ bhaddake kappe ayaṃbuddho bhavissati.
13 Ahu Kapilavhaye ramme . . . pe . . . . [xx. 14]
. . . pe . . . . [iv. 13]
14 Tassâpi vacanaṃ sutvâ bhiyyo cittaṃ pasâdayiṃ
uttarivatam adhiṭṭhâsiṃ dasapâramipûriyâ.
15 Sabbaññutaṃ gavesanto dânaṃ datvâ naruttame
ohâyâhaṃ mahârajjaṃ pabbajiṃ tassa santike.
16 Nagaraṃ Sobhavatî nâma Sobho nâmâsi khattiyo
vasati tattha nagare sambuddhassa mahâkulaṃ.

17 Brâhmaṇo Yaññadatto ca âsi buddhassa so pitâ
Uttarâ nâma janikâ Koṇâgamanassa satthuno.
18 Tîṇivassasahassâni agâraṃ ajjha so vasi
Tusita-Santusita-Santuṭṭhâ tayo pâsâdamuttamâ.
19 Anûnasoḷasasahassâni nâriyo samalaṅkatâ
Rucigattâ nâma nârî Satthavâho nâma atrajo.
20 Nimitte caturo disvâ hatthiyânena nikkhami
chamâsaṃ padhânacâram acari purisuttamo.
21 Brahmunâ yâcito santo Koṇâgamano nâyako
vatti cakkaṃ mahavîro Migadâye naruttamo.
22 Bhîyyo so Uttaro nâma ahesuṃ aggasâvakâ
Soṭṭhijo nâm' upaṭṭhâko Konâgamanassa satthuno.
23 Samuddâ ca Uttarâ c' eva ahesuṃ aggasâvikâ
bodhi tassa bhagavato Udambaro ti vuccati.
24 Uggo ca Somadevo ca ahesuṃ aggupaṭṭhakâ
Sîvalâ c' eva Sâmâ ca ahesuṃ aggupaṭṭhikâ.
25 Uccatarena so buddho tiṃsahatthasamuggato
ukkâmukkhe yathâ kambu evaṃ raṃsîhi maṇḍito.
26 Tiṃsavassasahassâni âyu buddhassa tâvade
tâvatâ tiṭṭhamâno so târesi janataṃ bahuṃ.
27 Dhammacetiṃ samussitvâ dhammadussavibhûsitaṃ
dhammapupphaguḷaṃ katvâ nibbuto so sasâvako.
28 Mahâvilâso tassa jano siridhammappakâsano
sabbaṃ samantarahitaṃ nanu rittâ sabbasaṅkhârâ.
29 Koṇâgamano sambuddho Pabbatârâmamhi nibbuto
dhâtuvitthârikaṃ âsi tesu tesu padesato ti.

KOṆÂGAMANASSA BHAGAVATO VAṂSA TEVÎSATIMO.

XXV.

KASSAPA THE TWENTY-FOURTH BUDDHA.

1 Koṇâgamanassa aparena sambuddho dvipaduttamo
Kassapo nâma nâmena dhammarâjâ pabhaṅkaro.
2 Sañchaḍḍitam kulamûlaṃ bahunaṃ pânabhojanaṃ
datvâna yâcake dânaṃ pûrayitvâna mânasaṃ
Usabho va âlakaṃ bhetvâ patto sambodhim uttamaṃ.
3 Dhammacakkappavattente Kassape lokanâyake
Vîsatikoṭisahassânaṃ paṭhamâbhisamayo ahu
4 Catumâsaṃ yadâ buddho loke carati cârikaṃ
Dasakoṭisahassânaṃ dutiyâbhisamayo ahu.
5 Yamakaṃ vikubbanaṃ katvâ ñâṇadhâtum pakittayi
pañcakoṭisahassânaṃ tatiyâbhisamayo ahu
6 Sudhamma-devapure ramme tattha dhammam pakâsayi
tîṇikotisahassânaṃ devânaṃ bodhayi jino.
.7 Naradevassa yakkhassa apare dhammadesane
etesânaṃ abhisamayâ gaṇanâto asaṅkheyyâ.
8 Tassâpi devadassa eko âsi samâgamo
khîṇâsavânaṃ vimalânaṃ santacittânaṃ tâdinaṃ.
9 Vîsatibhikkhusahassânaṃ tadâ âsi samâgamo
abhikkantabhagavantânaṃ hirisîlena tâdinaṃ.
10 Ahaṃ tadâ mâṇavako Jotipâlo ti vissuto
ajjhâyako mantadharo tiṇṇaṃ vedânapâragû.
11 Lakkhaṇe itihâse ca saddhamme pâramiṅgato
bhummantalikkhe kusalo katavijjo anâvayo.
12 Kassapassa bhagavato Ghaṭikâro nâm' upaṭṭhako
Sagâravo Sappatisso, nibbuto tatiye phale.
13 Âdâya maṃ Ghaṭikâro upagañchi Kassapaṃ jinaṃ
tassa dhammaṃ suṇitvâna pabbajiṃ tassa santike.
14 Âraddhaviriyo hutvâ vattâvattesu kovido
na kvâci parihâyâmi pûremi jinasâsanaṃ.
15 Yâvatâ buddhabhaṇitaṃ navaṅgaṃ satthusâsanaṃ
sabbaṃ pariyâpuṇitvâna sobhayiṃ jinasâsanaṃ.
16 Mama acchariyaṃ disvâ so pi buddho viyâkari
imamhi bhaddake kappe ayaṃ buddho bhavissati.

17 Ahu Kapilavhaye ramme nikkhamitvâ Tathâgato
padhânaṃ padahitvâna katvâna dukkarakâriyaṃ
. . . pe . . . . [iv. 13]
18 Ajapâlarukkhamûle nisîditvâ Tathâgato
tattha pâyâsam paggayha Nerañjaraṃ upehiti
19 Nerañjarâya tîramhi pâyâsaṃ paribhuñjiya
paṭiyattavaramaggena bodhimûlam upehiti.
20 Tato padakkhiṇaṃ katvâ bodhimaṇḍaṃ naruttamo
aparâjitanîyaṭṭhâne bodhipallaṅkamuttame.
21 Pallaṅkena nisîditvâ bujjhissati mahâyaso
imassa janikâ mâtâ Mâyâ nâmâ bhavissati
pitâ Suddhodano nâma ayaṃ hessati Gotamo.
22 Anâsavâ vîtarâgâ santacittâ samâhitâ
Kolito Upatisso ca aggâ hessanti sâvakâ.
23 Ânando nâm' upaṭṭhâko upaṭṭhissati taṃ jinaṃ
Khemâ Uppalavannâ ca aggâ hessanti sâvikâ
24 Anâsavâ santacittâ vîtarâgâ samâhitâ.
bodhi tassa bhagavato Assattho ti pavuccati.
25 Citto ca Hatthâḷavako aggâ hessant' upaṭṭhakâ.
Nandamâtâ ca Uttarâ aggâ hessant' upaṭṭhikâ.
26 Idaṃ sutvâna vacanam asamassa mahesino
âmoditâ naramarû buddha-bîjaṅkuro ayaṃ
27 Ukkutthi-saddâ pavattanti appoṭhenti hassanti ca
Katanjalî namassanti dasasahassî sadevakâ.
28 Yad' imassa lokanâthassa virajjhissâma sâsanaṃ
anûgatamhi addhâne hessâma sammukhâ imaṃ.
29 Yathâ manussâ nadiṃ tarantâ paṭitittham virajjhiya
heṭṭhâ titthe gahetvâna uttaranti mahânadiṃ.
30 Evam eva mayaṃ sabbe yadi muñcâm' imaṃ jinaṃ
anâgatamhi addhâne hessâma sammukhâ imaṃ.
31 Tassâpi vacanaṃ sutvâ bhîyyo cittam pasâdayiṃ
uttarivatam adhiṭṭhâsim dasapâramipûriyâ.
32 Evam ahaṃ saṃsaretvâ parivajjanto anâcâraṃ
dukkarañ ca kataṃ mayhaṃ bodhiyâ yeva kâraṇâ.
33 Nagaraṃ Bârâṇasi nâma Kiki nâm' âsi khattiyo
vasati tattha nagare sambuddhassa mahâkulaṃ
34 Brâhmaṇo Brahmadatto ca âsi buddhassa so pitâ
Dhanavatî nâma janikâ Kassapassa mahesino.

35 Duve vassasahassâni agâraṃ ajjha so vasi
Haṃso Yaso Sirinando tayo pâsâdamuttamâ.
36 Tisoḷassa-sahassâni nârivo samalaṅkatâ
Sunandâ nâma sâ nârî Vijitaseno nâma atrajo.
37 Nimitte caturo disvâ pâsâdenâbhinikkhami
sattâhaṃ padhânacâraṃ acari purisuttamo.
38 Brahmunâ yâcito santo Kassapo lokanâyako
vatti cakkaṃ mahâvîro Migadâye naruttamo.
39 Tisso ca Bhâradvâjo ca ahesum aggasâvakâ
Sabbamitto upaṭṭhâko Kassapassa mahesino.
40 Anuḷâ ca Uruveḷâ ca ahesum aggasâvikâ
bodhi tassa bhagavato Nigrodho ti pavuccati.
41 Sumaṅgalo Ghaṭikâro ca ahesum aggupaṭṭhakâ
Vijitasenâ ca Bhaddâ ca ahesum aggupaṭṭhikâ.
42 Uccatarena so buddho vîsatiratanamuggato
vijjulaṭṭhi va âkâse cando va gahapûrito.
43 Vîsavassasahassâni âyu tassa mahesino
tâvatâ tiṭṭhamâno so târesi janataṃ bahuṃ.
44 Dhammatalâkaṃ mâpetvâ sîlaṃ datvâ vilepanaṃ
dhammadussaṃ nivâsetvâ dhammamâlaṃ virâjiya
45 Dammavimalam âdâsaṃ ṭhapayitvâ mahâjane
keci nibbânaṃ patthentâ passantu me alaṅkaraṃ.
46 Sîlakañcukaṃ datvâna jhânakavacavammikaṃ
dhammacammaṃ pârupetvâ datvâ sannâham uttamaṃ.
47 Satiphalakaṃ datvâna tikhiṇañâṇakuntimaṃ
dhamma-khaggavaraṃ datvâ sîla-saṃsaggamaddanaṃ
48 Tevijjâbhûsaṃ datvâna âveḷaṃ caturo phale
chaḷabhiññâbharaṇaṃ datvâ dhammapupphapilandhanaṃ
49 Saddhammapaṇḍaraṃ chattaṃ datvâ pâpanivâraṇaṃ
mâpetvâ abhayaṃ pupphaṃ nibbuto so sasâvako.
50 Eso hi sammâ sambuddho appameyyo durâsado
eso hi dhammaratano svâkhyâto ehipassiko.
51 Eso hi saṅgharatano suppaṭipanno anuttaro
sabbaṃ samantarahitaṃ nanu rittâ sabbasaṅkharâ.
52 Mahâkassapo jino satthâ Setavyârâmamhi nibbuto
tatth' eva tassa jinathûpo yojanubbedhamuggato ti.

KASSAPASSA BHAGAVATO VAMSO CATUVÎSATIMO.

XXVI.

THE HISTORY OF GOTAMA BUDDHA.

1 Aham etarahi buddho Gotamo sakyavaḍḍhano
padhânaṃ padahitvâna patto sambodhim uttamaṃ.
2 Brahmunâ yâcito santo dhammacakkaṃ pavattayiṃ
aṭṭhârasannaṃ koṭînaṃ paṭhamâbhisamayo ahu.
3 Tato parañ ca desento naradevasamâgamo
gaṇanâya na vattabbo dutiyâbhisamayo ahu.
4 Idh' evâhaṃ etarahi ovâdiṃ mama atrajaṃ
gaṇanâya na vattabbo tatiyâbhisamayo ahu.
5 Eko va sannipâto me sâvakânaṃ mahesinaṃ
aḍḍhateḷasasatânaṃ bhikkhunâsi samâgamo.
6 Virocamâno vimalo bhikkhusaṅghassa majjhato
dadâmi patthitaṃ sabbaṃ maṇî va sabbakâmado.
7 Phalam âkaṅkhamânaṃ bhavacchandajahesinaṃ
catusaccaṃ pakâsesi anukampâya pâṇinaṃ.
8 Dasavîsasahassânaṃ dhammâbhisamayo ahu
ekadvinnaṃ abhisamayo gaṇanâto asaṅkheyyo.
9 Vitthârikaṃ bahujaññaṃ iddhaṃ phîtaṃ suphullitaṃ
idha mayhaṃ Sakyamunino sâsanaṃ suvisodhitaṃ.
10 Anâsavâ vîtarâgâ santacittâ samâhitâ
bhikkhû nekasatâ sabbe parivârenti maṃ sadâ.
11 Idâni ye etarahi jahanti mânusaṃ bhavaṃ
appattamânasâ sekhâ te bhikkhû viññû garahitâ
12 Ariyañjasaṃ thomayantâ sadâ dhammaratâ janâ
bujjhissanti satimanto saṃsârasaritâ narâ.
13 Nagaraṃ Kapilavatthu me râjâ Suddhodano pitâ
mayhaṃ janettikâ mâtâ Mâyâ devî ti vuccati.
14 Ekûnatiṃsavassâni agâram ajjh' ahaṃ vasiṃ
Râmo Surâmo Subhato tayo pâsâdamuttamâ.
15 Cattârîsasahassâni nâriyo samalaṅkatâ
Bhaddakaccâ nâma nârî Râhulo nâma atrajo.
16 Nimitte caturo disvâ assayânena nikkhamiṃ
Chabbassaṃ padhânacâraṃ acari dukkaraṃ ahaṃ.

17 Bârâṇasî Isipatane cakkaṃ pavattitaṃ mayâ
aham Gotamasambuddho saraṇaṃ sabbapâṇinaṃ.
18 Kolito Upatisso ca dve bhikkhû aggasâvakâ
Ânando nâm' upatthâko santikâvacaro mama.
19 Khemâ Uppalavaṇṇâ ca bhikkhunî aggasâvikâ
Citto ca Hatthâḷavako aggupaṭṭhâkupâsakâ
20 Nandamâtâ ca Uttarâ aggupaṭṭhikupâsikâ.
Ahaṃ Assatthamûlamhi patto sambodhim uttamaṃ.
21 Byâmappabhâ sadâ mayhaṃ soḷasahatthamuggato
appaṃ vassasataṃ âyu idân' etarahi vijjati.
22 Tâvatâ tiṭṭhamâno 'haṃ târemi janataṃ bahuṃ.
ṭhapayitvâ na'dhammokkaṃ pacchimajanabodhanaṃ.
23 Aham pi na cirass' eva saddhiṃ sâvakasaṅghato
idh' eva parinibbissaṃ aggi vâhârasaṅkhayâ.
24 Tâni ca atulatejâni imâni ca dasabalâni
ayañ ca guṇavaradeho dvattiṃsalakkhaṇâcito
25 Asadisâ pabhâsetvâ sataraṃsî va chappabhâ
sabbâ samantarahessanti nanu rittâ sabbasaṅkhârâti.

GOTAMASSA BHAGAVATO VAṂSO PAÑCAVÎSATIMO.

XXVII.

LIST OF THE BUDDHAS.

1 Aparimeyye ito kappe caturo âsuṃ vinâyakâ
Taṇhaṅkaro Medhaṅkaro atho pi Saraṇaṅkaro
Dîpaṅkaro ca sambuddho ekakappamhi te jinâ.
2 Dîpaṅkarassa aparena Koṇḍaññassa nâma nâyako
Eko va ekakappamhi târesi janataṃ bahuṃ.
3 Dîpaṅkarassa bhagavato Koṇḍaññassa ca satthuno
etesaṃ antarâ kappâ gaṇanâto asaṅkhiyâ.
4 Kondaññassa aparena Maṅgalo nâma nâyako
tesam pi antarâ kappâ gaṇanâto asaṅkhiyâ.
5 Maṅgalo ca Sumano ca Revato Sobhito muni
te pi buddhâ ekakappe cakkhumanto pabhaṅkarâ.

6 Sobhitassa aparena Anomadassî mahâyaso
tesam pi antarâ kappâ gaṇanâto asaṅkhiyâ.
7 Anomadassî Padumo Nârado câpi nâyako
te pi buddhâ ekakappe tamantakârakâ munî
8 Nâradassa aparena Padumuttaro nâma nâyako
ekakappamhi uppanno târesi janataṃ bahuṃ.
9 Nâradassa bhagavato Padumuttarassa satthuno
tesam pi antarâ kappâ gaṇanâto asaṅkihyâ.
10 Kappasatasahassamhi eko âsi mahâmuni
Padumuttaro lokavidû âhutînaṃ paṭiggaho.
11 Tiṃsakappasahassamhi duve âsiṃsu nâyakâ
Sumedho ca Sujâto ca oraso Padumuttaro.
12 Aṭṭhârase ito kappasate tayo âsiṃsu nâyakâ
Piyadassî Atthadassî Dhammadassî ca nâyakâ.
13 Oraso ca Sujâtassa sambuddhâ dvipaduttamâ
ekakappamhi sambuddhâ loke appaṭipuggalâ.
14 Catunavute ito kappe eko âsi mahâmuni
Siddhattho so lokavidû sallagatto anuttaro.
15 Dve navute ito kappe duve âsiṃsu nâyakâ
Tisso Phusso ca sambuddhâ asamâ appaṭipuggalâ.
16 Ekanavute ito kappe Vipassî nâma nâyako
so pi buddho kâruṇiko satte moceṣi bandhanâ.
17 Ekatiṃse ito kappe duve âsiṃsu nâyakâ
Sikkhî ca Vessabhû c' eva asamâ appaṭipuggalâ.
18 Imamhi bhaddake kappe tayo âsiṃsu nâyakâ
Kakusandho Koṇâgamano Kassapo câpi nâyako.[1]
19 Ahaṃ etarahi sambuddho Metteyo câpi hessati
Ete p' ime pañca buddhâ dhîrâ lokânukampakâ.
20 Etesaṃ dhammarâjûnaṃ aññesaṃ nekakoṭinaṃ
âcikkhitvâna taṃ maggaṃ nibbutâ te sasâvakâ ti.

BUDDHAPAKIṆṆAKKHAṆḌAṂ NIṬṬHITAṂ.

[1] Here the *Buddhavaṃsa* rightly ends :—
"Aparimeyye ito kappe . . . pe . . . [xxvii. 1] âdinâ atthârasagâthâ saṅgîtikârakehi ṭhapitâ nigamanagâthâ veditabbâ. Sesagâthâsu sabbattha pâkaṭam evâ ti."—(Madhuratthavilâsinî).

XXVIII.

THE DISTRIBUTION OF BUDDHA'S RELICS.

1 Mahâ Gotamo jinavaro Kusinârâmamhi nibbuto•
dhâtuvitthârikam âsi tesu tesu padesato ti.
2 Eko Ajâtasathussa, eko Vesâliyâ pure,
eko Kapilavatthumhi, eko ca Allakappake,
3 Eko ca Râmagâmamhi, eko ca Veṭhadîpake,
eko Pâveyyake Malle, eko ca Kusinârake.
4 Kumbhassa thûpaṃ kâresi brâhmâṇo Doṇasavhayo
Aṅgârathûpaṃ kâresuṃ Moriyâ tuṭṭhamânasâ.
5 Aṭṭha sarîrikâ thûpâ, navamo kumbhacetiyo
Aṅgârathûpo dasamo tadâ yeva patiṭṭhito.[1]
6 Ekâ dâthâ Tidasapure, ekâ Nâgapure ahu,
ekâ Gandhâravisaye, ekâ Kâliṅgarâjino.
7 Cattâḷîsasamâdantâ kesâ lomâ ca sabbaso
devâ hariṃsu ekekaṃ cakkavâlaparamparâ.
8 Vajirâyaṃ bhagavato patto daṇḍañ ca cîvaraṃ
nivâsanaṃ Kusaghare paccattharaṇaṃ Kapilavhaye
9 Pâṭaliputtanagare karakaṃ kâya-bandhanaṃ
Campâyaṃ udaka-sâṭikâ uṇṇalomañ ca Kosale.
10 Kâsâvañ ca Brahmaloke veṭhanaṃ Tidase pure
pâsâṇake padaṃ seṭṭhaṃ yañ câpi accutipadaṃ.
nisîdanaṃ Avantipure raṭṭhe attharaṇaṃ tadâ.
11 Araṇî ca Mithilâyaṃ Vedehi parisâvanaṃ

[1] The Phayre MS. here inserts the following lines:

1 Uṇhissaṃ caturo dâthâ akkhagâ dve ca dhâtuyo
asambhinnâ imâ sattâ sesâ bhinnâ va dhâtuyo
2 Mahantâ muggamattâ ca majjhimâ bhinnataṇḍulâ
khuddakâ sâ sapamattâ nânâvaṇṇâ ca dhâtuyo
3 Mahantâ suvaṇṇavaṇṇâ muttavaṇṇâ ca majjhimâ
khuddakâ makulavaṇṇâ ca soḷasadoṇimattikâ
4 Mahantâ pañca nâḷiyo nâḷiyo pañca majjhimâ
khuddakâ ca chanâḷi ca etâ sabbâpi dhâtuyo
5 Uṇhissaṃ Sîhale dîpe Brahmaloke ca vâmakaṃ
Sîhale dakkhiṇakkhañ ca sabbâ p' etâ patiṭṭhitâ.

vâsisûcigharañ câpi Indaraṭṭhe pure tadâ.
12 Parikkhâraṃ avasesaṃ janapade aparantake
paribhuttâni muninâ akaṃsu manujâ tadâ.
13 Dhâtuvitthârikaṃ âsi Gotamassa mahesino
pâṇinam anukampâya ahû porânikâ tadâ ti.[1]

DHÂTUBHÂJANIYAKATHÂ NIṬṬHITÂ.

BUDDHAVAṂSO NIṬṬHITO.

Ph. adds the following lines:—

Revato Sobhito buddho Padumo dvipaduttamo
Sumedho Atthadassî ca Phusso ca Vessabhû jino
Koṇâgamano Gotamo navannaṃ dhâtû vitthatâ
soḷasannam avitthârâ te pi vandâmi dhâtuyo
Sahassadvisatâ gâthâ catusaṭṭhi ca piṇḍato
Padhânamâdipeyyâle nimuggâ dasa gâthakâ
Ahu Kappilapeyyâle nimuggâ pana cuddasa.

[1] See *Mahâparinibbânasutta*, ed. Childers, pp. 70, 71.

CARIYÂ-PIṬAKA

CARIYÂ-PIṬAKA.

Namo tassa bhagavato arahato sammâsambuddhassa.

BOOK I.

DÂNAPÂRAMITÂ.

I.

THE STORY OF AKATTI.

1 Kappe ca satasahasse caturo ca asaṅkheyye
etth' antare yaṃ caritaṃ sabban taṃ bodhipâcanaṃ.
2 Atîtakappe caritaṃ ṭhapayitvâ bhavâbhave
imamhi kappe caritaṃ pavakkhissaṃ suṇohi me.
3 Yadâ âhaṃ brahâraññe suññe vivinakânane
ajjhogâhetvâ viharâmi Akatti nâma tâpaso.
4 Tadâ maṃ tapatejena santatto Tidivâdhibhû
dhârento brâhmaṇavaṇṇaṃ bhikkhâya maṃ upâgami.
5 Pavanâ âbhaṭaṃ paṇṇaṃ atelañ ca aloṇikaṃ
mama dvâre ṭhitaṃ disvâ sakaṭâhena âkiriṃ.
6 Tassa datvân' ahaṃ paṇṇaṃ nikkujjitvâna bhâjanaṃ
pun' esanaṃ jahitvâna pâvisiṃ paṇṇasâlakaṃ.
7 Dutiyam pi tatiyam pi upagañchi mam' antikaṃ
akampito anolaggo evam eva adâs' ahaṃ.
8 Na me tappaccayâ atthi sarîrasmiṃ vivaṇṇiyaṃ
pîtisukhena ratiyâ vîtinâmemi taṃ divaṃ.
9 Yadi mâsam pi dve mâsaṃ dakkhiṇeyyaṃ varaṃ labhe
akampito anolîno dadeyyaṃ dânam uttamaṃ.
10 Na tassa dânaṃ dadamâno yasaṃ lâbhañ ca patthayiṃ
sabbaññutaṃ patthayâno tâni kammâni âcarin ti.

AKATTICARIYAṂ PAṬHAMAṂ.

II.

THE STORY OF SAṄKHA.

1 Punâparaṃ yadâ homi brâhmaṇo Saṅkhasavhayo
mahâsamuddaṃ taritukâmo upagacchâmi paṭṭanaṃ.
2 Tattha adassim paṭipathe sayambhum apparâjitaṃ
kantâraddhânaṃ paṭipannaṃ tattâya kaṭhinabhûmiyâ.
3 Tam ahaṃ paṭipathe disvâ imam atthaṃ vicintayiṃ
idaṃ khettaṃ anupattaṃ puññakâmassa jantuno.
4 Yathâpi kassako puriso khettaṃ disvâ mahâgamaṃ
tattha bîjaṃ na ropeti na so dhaññena atthiko
5 Evam evâhaṃ puññakâmo disvâ khettavaruttamaṃ
yadi tattha kâraṃ na karomi nâhaṃ puññena atthiko.
6 Yathâ amacco muddikâmo rañño antepure jane
na deti tesaṃ dhanadhaññaṃ muddito parihâyati.
7 Evam evâhaṃ puññakâmo vipulaṃ disvâna dakkhiṇaṃ
yadi tassa dânam na dadâmi parihâyissâmi puññato.
8 Evâhaṃ cintayitvâna orohitvâ upâhanâ
tassa pâdâni vanditvâ adâsiṃ chattupâhanaṃ
9 Ten' evâhaṃ sataguṇato sukhumâlo sukhe ṭhito
api ca dânaṃ paripûrento evaṃ tassa adâs' ahan ti.

SAṄKHACARIYAṂ DUTIYAṂ.

III.

THE STORY OF DHANAÑJAYA.

1 Punâparaṃ yadâ homi Indapatthe puruttame
râjâ Dhanañjayo nâma kusale dasah' upâgato.
2 Kâliṅgaraṭṭha-visayâ brâhmaṇâ upagañchuṃ maṃ
âyâcuṃ maṃ hatthinâgaṃ dhaññaṃ maṅgalasammataṃ.
3 Avuṭṭhiko janapado dubbhikkho châtako mahâ
dadâhi pavaraṃ nâgaṃ nîlaṃ Añjanasavhayaṃ.

4 Na me yâcakam anupatte paṭikkhepo anucchavo
mâ me bhijji samâdânaṃ dassâmi vipulaṃ gajaṃ.
5 Nâgaṃ gahetvâ soṇḍâyaṃ bhiṅkâre ratanâmaye
jalaṃ hatthe âkiritvâ brâhmaṇânaṃ adaṃ gajaṃ.
6 Tasmiṃ nâge padinnamhi amaccâ etad abravuṃ :—
kinnu tuyhaṃ varaṃ nâgaṃ yâcakânaṃ padassasi ?
7 Dhaññaṃ maṅgalasampannaṃ saṅgâmavijayuttamaṃ
tasmiṃ nâge padinnamhi kin te rajjaṃ karissatî ti ?
8 Rajjam pi me dade sabbaṃ sarîraṃ dajjam attano
sabbaññutam piyaṃ mayhaṃ tasmâ nâgaṃ adâs' ahan ti.

ITI KURUDHAMMACARIYAṂ TATIYAṂ.

IV.

THE STORY OF SUDASSANA.

1 Kusâvatimhi nagare yadâ âsi mahîpati
Mahâsudassano nâma cakkavattî mahabbhalo.
2 Tatthâhaṃ divase tikkhattuṃ ghosâpemi tahiṃ tahiṃ
ko kiṃ icchati pattheti kassa kiṃ dîyatu dhanaṃ ?
3 Ko châtako ko tasito ko mâlaṃ ko vilepanaṃ
nânârattâni vatthâni ko naggo paridahissati ?
ko pathe chattam âdeti kopâhanâ mudusabhâ ?
4 Iti sâyañ ca pâto ca ghosâpemi tahiṃ tahiṃ
na taṃ dasasu ṭhânesu na pi ṭhânasatesu vâ.
5 Anekasataṭṭhânesu paṭiyattam yâcake dhanaṃ
divâ vâ yadi vâ ratti yadi eti vanîpako.
6 Laddhâ yadicchikaṃ bhogaṃ purahattho va gacchati
evarûpaṃ mahâdânaṃ adâsiṃ yâvajîvikaṃ.
7 Na pâhaṃ dessaṃ dhanaṃ dammi pi n' atthi nicayo mayi
yathâpi âturo nâma rogato parimuttiyâ.
8 Dhanena vajjaṃ tappetvâ rogato parimuccati
tath' evâhaṃ jânamâno paripûretum asesato
9 Ûnadhanaṃ pûrayituṃ demi dânaṃ vanîpake
nirâlayo apaccâyo sambodhimanupattiyâ ti.

MAHÂSUDASSANACARIYAṂ CATUTTHAṂ.

V.

THE STORY OF GOVINDA.

1 Punâparaṃ yadâ homi sattarâjapurohito
pûjito naradevehi Mahâgovindo brâhmaṇo.
2 Tadâhaṃ sattarajjesu yaṃ me âsi upâyanaṃ
tena demi mahâdânaṃ akkhobbhaṃ sâgarûpamaṃ.
3 Na me dessaṃ dhanadhaññaṃ pi n' atthi niccayo mayi
sabbaññutam piyaṃ mayhaṃ tasmâ demi varaṃ dhanan ti.

MAHÂGOVINDACARIYAṂ PAÑCAMAṂ.

VI.

THE STORY OF NIMI.

1 Punâparaṃ yadâ homi Mithilâyam puruttame
Nimi nâma mahârâjâ paṇḍito kusalatthiko
2 Tadâhaṃ mâpayitvâna catusâlaṃ catumukhaṃ
tattha dânaṃ pavattesiṃ miga-pakkhi-nara-nârinam
3 Acchâdanañ ca sayanañ ca annapânañ ca bhojanaṃ
Abbhocchinnaṃ karitvâna mahâdânaṃ pavattayiṃ.
4 Yathâpi sevako sâmiṃ dhanahetum upâgato
kâyena vâcâ manasâ ârâdhanîyam esati
5 Tath' evâhaṃ sabbabhave pariyesissâmi bodhijaṃ
dânena satte tappetvâ icchâmi bodhim uttaman ti.

NIMIRÂJACARIYAṂ CHAṬṬHAMAṂ.

VII.

THE STORY OF CANDAKUMÂRA.

1 Punâparaṃ yadâ homi Ekarâjassa atrajo
nagare Pupphavatiyâ kumâro Candasavhayo
2 Tadâhaṃ yajanâ mutto nikkhanto yaññavâṭako
samvegaṃ janayitvâna mahâdânaṃ pavattayiṃ.
3 Nâham pivâmi khâdâmi na pi bhuñjâmi bhojanaṃ
dakkhiṇeyyam adatvâna api chappañca rattiyo.
4 Yathâpi vâṇijo nâma katvâna bhaṇḍasañcayaṃ
yattha lâbho mahâ hoti tatthâharati bhaṇḍakaṃ.
5 Tath' eva sakabhuttâpi pare dinnaṃ mahapphalaṃ
tasmâ parassa dâtabbaṃ satabhâgo bhavissati.
6 Etam atthavasaṃ ñatvâ demi dânaṃ bhavâbhave
na paṭikkamâmi dânato sambodhimanupattiyâ ti.

CANDAKUMÂRACARIYAṂ SATTAMAṂ.

VIII.

THE STORY OF SIVI.

1 Ariṭṭhasavhaye nagare Sivi nâmâsi khattiyo
nisajja pâsâdavare evaṃ cintes' ahan tadâ.
2 Yaṃ kiñci mânusam dânaṃ adinnaṃ me na vijjati
yo pi yâceyya maṃ cakkhuṃ dadeyyaṃ avikampito.
3 Mama saṅkappam aññâya Sakko devânam issaro
nisinno devaparisâya idaṃ vacanam abravi :—
4 Nisajja pâsâdavare Sivi-râjâ mahiddhiko
cintento vividhaṃ dânaṃ adeyyaṃ so na passati.
5 Tathaṃ nu vitathan n' etaṃ handa vimaṃsayâmi taṃ
muhuttaṃ âgameyyâtha yâva jânâmi taṃ manan ti.
6 Pavedhamâno phalitasiro valitagatto jarâturo
andhavaṇṇo va hutvâna râjânaṃ upasaṅkami.

7 So tadâ paggahetvâna vâmaṃ dakkhiṇabâhu ca
sirasmiṃ añjaliṃ katvâ idaṃ vacanam abravi :—
8 Yâcâmi taṃ mahârâja dhammikaraṭṭhavaḍḍhanaṃ
tava dânaratâ kitti uggatâ devamânuse
9 Ubho pi nettâ nayanâ andhâ upahatâ mama
ekaṃ me nayanaṃ dehi tvam pi ekena yâpayâ ti.
10 Tassâhaṃ vacanaṃ sutvâ haṭṭho saṃviggamânaso
katañjalî vedajâto idaṃ vacanam abraviṃ :—
11 Idânâhaṃ cintayitvâna pâsâdato idh' âgato
tvaṃ mama cittam aññâya nettaṃ yâcitum âgato.
12 Aho me mânasaṃ siddhaṃ saṅkappo paripûrito
adinnapubbâṃ dânavaraṃ ajja dassâmi yâcake.
13 Ehi Sîvaka uṭṭhehi mâ dantayi mâ pavedhayi
ubho pi nayane dehi uppâṭetvâ va tibbake.
14 Tato so codito mayhaṃ Sîvako vacanaṃ karo
uddharitvâna pâdâsi tâlamiñjaṃ va yâcake.
15 Dadamânassa dentassa dinnadânassa me sato
cittassa aññathâ n' atthi bodhiyâ yeva kâraṇâ.
16 Na me dessâ ubho cakkhû attâ na me na dessiyo
sabbaññutam piyaṃ mayhaṃ tasmâ cakkhuṃ adâs' ahan ti.

SIVIRÂJACARIYAṂ AṬṬHAMAṂ.

IX.

THE STORY OF VESSANTARA.

1 Yâ me ahosi janikâ Phussatî nâma khattiyâ
sâ atîtâsu jâtisu Sakkassa ca mahesiyâ.
2 Tassâ âyukkhayaṃ disvâ devindo etad abravi :—
dadâmi te dasa vare varaṃ bhadde yad icchasî ti.
3 Evaṃ vuttâ ca sâ devî Sakkaṃ purindam abravi :—
kinnu me aparâdh' atthi kinnu dessâ ahan tava
rammâ câvesi maṃ ṭhânâ vâto va dharaṇiṃ ruhan ti?
4 Evaṃ vutte ca so Sakko puna tassedam abravi :—
na c' eva te kataṃ pâpaṃ na ca me tvam asi appiyâ.

5 Ettakaṃ yeva te âyuṃ cavanakâlo bhavissati
paṭigganha mayâ dinne vare dasa varuttame ti.
6 Sakkena sâ dinnavarâ tuṭṭhahaṭṭhâ pamoditâ
mamam abbhantaraṃ katvâ Phusatî dasa vare varî.
7 Tato cutâ sâ Phusatî khattiye upapajjatha
Jetuttaramhi nagare Sañjayena samâgami.
8 Yadâhaṃ Phusatiyâ kucchiṃ okkanto piyamâtuyâ
mamạ tejena me mâtâ sadâ dânaratâ ahu.
9 Ádhane âture jiṇṇe yâcake paṭṭhike jane
samaṇabrâhmaṇe khîṇe deti dânaṃ akiñcane.
10 Dasa mâse dhârayitvâna karonte purapadakkhiṇaṃ
Vessânaṃ vîthiyâ majjhe janesi Phusatî mamaṃ.
11 Na mayhaṃ mettikaṃ nâmaṃ na pi mettikasambhavaṃ
jâto 'mhi Vessavîthiyâ tasmâ Vessantaro ahu.
12 Yadâhaṃ dârako homi jâtiyâ aṭṭhavassiko
tadâ nisajja pâsâde dânaṃ dâtuṃ vicintayiṃ.
13 Hadayaṃ dadeyyaṃ cakkhuṃ maṃsam pi ruhiram pi ca
dadeyyaṃ kâyaṃ yâcetvâ yadi koci yâcaye mamaṃ.
14 Sabhâvam cintayantassa akampitam asaṇṭhitaṃ
akampi tattha paṭhavî Sineruvanavaṭaṃsakâ.
15 Addhaddhamâse paṇṇarase puṇṇamâse uposathe
paccayaṃ nâgam âruyha dânaṃ dâtuṃ upâgami.
16 Kâliṅgaraṭṭhavisayâ brâhmaṇâ upagañchuṃ maṃ
âyâcuṃ maṃ hatthinâgaṃ dhaññamaṅgalasammataṃ.
17 Avuṭṭhito janapado dubbhikkho châtako mahâ
dadâhi pavaraṃ nâgaṃ sabbasetaṃ gajuttamaṃ.
18 Dadâmi na vikampâmi yaṃ maṃ yâcanti brâhmaṇâ
santaṃ nappaṭiguhâmi dâne me ramatî mano.
19 Na me yâcakam anuppatte paṭikkhepo anucchavo
mâ me bhijji samâdânam dassâmi vipulaṃ gajaṃ.
20 Nâgaṃ gahetvâ soṇḍâya bhiṅkâre ratanâmaye
. . . pe . . . . [p. 75, l. 5]
21 Punâparaṃ dadantassa sabbasetaṃ gajuttamaṃ
tadâpi paṭhavî kampi Sineruvanavaṭaṃsakâ.
22 Tassa nâgassa dânena Sivayo kuddhâ samâgatâ
pabbâjesuṃ sakâ raṭṭhâ Vaṅkaṃ gacchatu pabbataṃ.
23 Tesaṃ niccubhamânânaṃ akampitam asaṇṭhitaṃ
mahâdânaṃ pavattetuṃ ekaṃ varam ayâcissaṃ.

24 Yâcitâ Sivayo sabbe ekaṃ varam adaṃsu me
âyâcayitvâ kaṇṇabheriṃ mahâdânaṃ dadâm' ahaṃ.
25 Ath' ettha vattati saddo tumulo bheravo mahâ
dânena maṃ nîharanti puna dânam dadâm' ahaṃ.
26 Hatthî asse rathe datvâ dâsî dâsaṃ gavan dhanaṃ
mahâdânaṃ daditvâna nagarâ nikkhamiṃ tadâ.
27 Nikkhamitvâna nagarâ nivattitvâ vilokite
tadâpi paṭhavî kampi Sineruvanavaṭaṃsakâ.
28 Catuvâhiṃ rathaṃ datvâ ṭhatvâ câtumahâpathe
ekâkiyo adutiyo Maddi-deviṃ idam abraviṃ :—
29 Tvaṃ Maddi Kaṅhaṃ gaṇhâhi lahukâ esâ kaniṭṭhakâ
Ahaṃ Jâliṃ gahessâmi garuko bhâtiko hi so.
30 Padumaṃ puṇḍarîkaṃ va Maddî Kaṇhâjinam aggahî
ahaṃ suvaṇṇabimbaṃ va Jâliṃ khattiyam aggahiṃ.
Jalaṃ hatthe âkiritvâ brâhmaṇânaṃ adaṃ gajaṃ.
31 Abhijâtâ sukhumâlâ khattiyâ caturo janâ
visamasamaṃ akkamantâ Vaṅkaṃ gacchâma pabbataṃ.
32 Ye keci manujâ yanti anumagge paṭipathe
maggan te paṭipucchâma kuhiṃ Vaṇkatapabbato ti.
33 Te tattha amhe passitvâ karuṇaṃ giram udîrayuṃ
dukkhan te paṭivedenti dûre Vaṅkatapabbato.
34 Yadi passanti pavane dârakâ phalite dume
tesaṃ phalânaṃ hetumhi uparodanti dârakâ.
35 Rodante dârake disvâ ubbidhâ vipulâ dumâ
sayam ev' oṇamitvâna upagacchanti dârake.
36 Idam acchariyaṃ disvâ abbhutaṃ lomahaṃsanaṃ
sâdhukâraṃ pavattesi Maddî sabbaṅgasobhanâ.
37 Accheraṃ tava lokasmiṃ abbhutaṃ lomahaṃsanaṃ
Vessantarassa tejena sayam ev' oṇatâ dumâ.
38 Saṅkhipiṃsu pathaṃ yakkhâ anukampâya dârake
nikkhantadivasen' eva Cetaraṭṭham upâgamuṃ.
39 Satthirâjasahassâni tadâ vasanti mâtulâ
sabbe pañjalikâ hutvâ rodamânâ upâgamuṃ.
40 Tattha vattetvâ sallâpaṃ Cetehi Cetaputtehi
te tato nikkhamitvâna Vaṅkaṃ agamuṃ pabbataṃ.
41 Âmantayitvâ devindo Vissukammaṃ mahiddhikaṃ :—
assamaṃ sukataṃ rammaṃ paṇṇasâlaṃ su-mâpaya.
42 Sakkassa vacanaṃ sutvâ Vissukammo mahiddhiko

assamaṃ sukataṃ rammaṃ paṇṇasâlaṃ sumâpayi.
43 Ajjhogâhetvâ pavanaṃ appasaddaṃ nirâkulaṃ
caturo janâ mayaṃ tattha vasâma pabbatantare.
44 Ahañ ca Maddî devî ca Jâlikaṇhâjinâ cubho
aññamaññaṃ sokanudâ vasâma-assame tadâ.
45 Dârake anurakkhanto asuñño homi assame
Maddî phalaṃ âharati poseti sâ tayo jane.
46 Pavane vasamânassa addhiko maṃ upâgami
âyâci puttake mayhaṃ Jâlikaṇhâjine cubho.
47 Yâcakam upagataṃ disvâ hâso me upapajjatha
ubho putte gahetvâna adâsi brâhmaṇe tadâ.
48 Sake putte cajantassa yâcake brâhmaṇe yadâ
tadâpi paṭhavî kampi Sineruvanavaṭaṃsakâ.
49 Punad eva Sakko oruyha hutvâ brâhmaṇasannibho
âyâci maṃ Maddideviṃ sîlavatiṃ patibbataṃ.
50 Maddiṃ hatthe gahetvâna udakañjaliṃ pûraya
pasannamanasaṅkappo tassa Maddim adâs' ahaṃ.
51 Maddiyâ dîyamânâya gagane devâ pamoditâ
tadâpi paṭhavî kampi Sineruvanavaṭaṃsakâ.
52 Jâlikaṇhâjinaṃ dhîtaṃ Maddideviṃ patibbataṃ
cajjamâno na cintesiṃ bodhiyâ yeva kâraṇâ.
53 Na me dessâ ubho puttâ Maddî devî na dessiyâ
sabbaññutam piyaṃ mayhaṃ tasmâ piye adâs' ahaṃ.
54 Punâparaṃ brahâraññe mâtâpitu samâgame
karuṇaṃ paridevante sallapante sukhaṃ dukkhaṃ
55 Hirottappena garunâ ubhinnaṃ upasaṅkami
tadâpi paṭhavî kampi Sineruvanavaṭaṃsakâ.
56 Punâparaṃ brahâraññâ nikkhamitvâ sañâtibhi
pavissâmi puraṃ rammaṃ Jetuttaraṃ puruttamaṃ.
57 Ratanâni satta vassiṃsu mahâmegho pavassatha
tadâpi paṭhavî kampi Sineruvanavaṭaṃsakâ.
58 Acetanâyaṃ paṭhavî aviññâya sukhaṃ dukkhaṃ
sâpi dânabalâ mayhaṃ sattakkhattuṃ pakampathâ ti.

VESSANTARACARIYAṂ NAVAMAṂ.

X.

THE STORY OF THE HARE.

1 Punâparaṃ yadâ homi sasako pavanacâriko
tiṇapaṇṇasâkaphalabhakkho paraheṭhanavivajjito.
2 Makkaṭo ca siṅgâlo ca uddapoto c' ahaṃ tadâ
vasâma ekasâmantâ sâyaṃ pâto padissare.
3 Ahaṃ te anusâsâmi kiriye kalyâṇapâpake
pâpâni parivajjetha kalyâṇe abhinivassatha.
4 Uposathamhi divase candaṃ disvâna pûritaṃ
etesaṃ tattha âcikkhi divaso ajj' uposatho.
5 Dânâni paṭiyâdetha dakkhiṇeyyassa dâtave
datvâ dânaṃ dakkhiṇeyyaṃ upavassath' uposathaṃ.
6 Te me sâdhû ti vatvâna yathâ satti yathâ balaṃ.
Dânâni paṭiyâdetvâ dakkhiṇeyyaṃ gavesiṃsuṃ.
7 Ahaṃ nisajja cintesi dânaṃ dakkhiṇ' anucchavaṃ
Yadi 'haṃ labhe dakkhiṇeyyaṃ kiṃ me dânam bhavissati?
8 Na me atthi tilâ muggâ mâsâ vâ taṇḍulâ ghataṃ
ahaṃ tiṇena yâpemi na sakkâ tiṇaṃ dâtave.
9 Yadi eti dakkhiṇeyyo bhikkhâya mama santike
dajjâham sakam attânaṃ na so tuccho gamissati.
10 Mama saṅkappam aññâya Sakko brâhmaṇavaṇṇinâ
âsayaṃ me upâgañchi dânavîmaṃsanâya me
11 Tam ahaṃ disvâna santuṭṭho idaṃ vacanam abraviṃ :—
sâdhu kho si anupatto ghâsahetu mam' antike.
12 Adinnapubbaṃ dânavaraṃ ajja dassâmi te ahaṃ
tuvaṃ sîlâguṇûpeto ayuttaṃ te paraheṭhanaṃ
13 Ehi aggiṃ padîpehi nânâkaṭṭhe samânaya
ahaṃ pacissam attânaṃ pakkaṃ tvaṃ bhakkhayissasî ti.
14 Sâdhû ti so haṭṭhamano nânâkaṭṭhe samânayi
mahantaṃ akâsi citakaṃ katvân' aṅgâragabbhakaṃ.
15 Aggiṃ tattha padîpeti yathâ so khippaṃ mahâbhave
phoṭetvâ rajagate gatte ekamantaṃ upâvisi.
16 Yadâ mahâkaṭṭhapañjo âditto dhûmam âyati
tad uppatitvâ papatiṃ majjhe jâlasikhantare

17 Yathâ sîtodakaṃ nâma paviṭṭhaṃ yassa kassaci
sameti daratham pariḷâhaṃ assâdaṃ deti pîti ca.
18 Tath' eva jalitaṃ aggiṃ paviṭṭhassa mamaṃ tadâ
sabbaṃ sameti darathaṃ yathâ sîtodakaṃ viya.
19 Chavicammaṃ maṃsaṃ nahâruṃ aṭṭhihadayabandhanaṃ
kevalaṃ sakalaṃ kâyaṃ brâhmaṇassa adâs' ahan ti.

SASAPAṆḌITACARIYAṂ DASAMAṂ.

20 Akatti brâhmaṇo, Saṅkho, Kururâjâ Dhanañjayo,
Mahâsudassano râjâ, Mahâgovindabrâhmaṇo.
21 Nimi, Candakumâro ca, Sivi, Vessantaro, Saso
Aham eva tadâ âsiṃ yo te dânavare adâ.
22 Ete dânaparikkhârâ ete dânassa pâramî
Jîvitaṃ yâcake datvâ idaṃ pâramî pûrayiṃ.
23 Bhikkhây' upagataṃ disvâ sakattânaṃ pariccajiṃ
dâne na me samo n' atthi esâ me dânapâramî ti.

DÂNAPÂRAMITÂ NIṬṬHITÂ.

Book II.

SÎLAPÂRAMITÂ.

I.

THE STORY OF THE WISE ELEPHANT.

1 Yadâ ahosi pavane kuñjaro mâtu posako
na tadâ atthi mahiyâ guṇena mama sâdiso.
2 Pavane disvâ vanacaro raññno maṃ paṭivedayi
tav' anucchavo mahârâja gajo vasati kânane.
3 Na tassa parikkhây' attho na pi âḷakakâsuyâ
samâgahite soṇḍâya sayam eva idh' ehiti.
4 Tassa taṃ vacanaṃ sutvâ râjâ pi tuṭṭhamânaso
pesesi hatthidamakaṃ chekâcariyaṃ susikkhitaṃ.
5 Gantvâna so hatthidamako adassa padumassare
bhisamûlaṃ uddharantaṃ yâpanatthâya mâtuyâ.
6 Viññâya me sîlaguṇaṃ lakkhaṇaṃ upadhârayi
ehi puttâ ti vatvâna mama soṇḍâya aggahi.
7 Yam me tadâ pâkatikaṃ sarîrânugataṃ balaṃ
ajja nâgasahassânaṃ balena samasâdisaṃ.
8 Yadi 'haṃ tesaṃ pakuppeyyaṃ upetaṃ gahaṇâya maṃ
paṭibalo bhave tesaṃ yâva rajjam pi mânusaṃ.
9 Api câhaṃ sîlarakkhâya sîlapâramipûriyâ
na karomi citte aññathattaṃ pakkhipantaṃ mam âlake.
10 Yadi te maṃ tattha koṭṭeyyuṃ pharasûhi tomarehi ca
n'eva tesaṃ pakuppeyyaṃ sîlakhaṇḍabhayâ mamâ ti.

SÎLAVANÂGACARIYAṂ PAṬHAMAṂ.

II.

THE STORY OF BHÛRIDATTA-SNAKE.

1 Punâparaṃ yadâ homi Bhûridatto mahiddhiko
Virûpakkhena mahâraññâ devalokam agañch' ahaṃ.
2 Tattha passitvâ 'haṃ deve ekantaṃ sukhasamappite
taṃ saggaṃ gamanatthâya sîlabbataṃ samâdayiṃ.
3 Sarîrakiccaṃ katvâna bhutvâ yâpanamattakaṃ
caturo aṅge adhiṭṭhâya semi vammikamuddhani.
4 Chaviyâ cammena maṃsena nahâru-aṭṭhikehi vâ
yassa etena karaṇîyaṃ dinnaṃ yeva harâtu so.
5 Saṃsito akataññunâ Âlampâno mam aggahi
peḷâya pakkhipetvâna kîḷeti maṃ tahiṃ tahiṃ.
6 Peḷâya pakkhipante pi sammaddante pi pâṇinâ
Âlampânena na kuppâmi sîlakhaṇḍabhayâ mama.
7 Sakajîvitapariccâgo tiṇato lahuko mama
sîlavîtikkamo mayhaṃ paṭhavî uppattanâ viya.
8 Nirantaraṃ jâtisataṃ cajeyyaṃ mama jîvitaṃ
n' eva sîlaṃ pabhindeyyaṃ catudîpâna hetu pi.
9 Api câhaṃ sîlarakkhâya sîlapâramipûriyâ
na karomi citte aññathattaṃ pakkhipantam pi peḷake ti.

BHÛRIDATTACARIYAṂ DUTIYAṂ.

III.

THE STORY OF CAMPEYYA-SNAKE.

1 Punâparaṃ yadâ homi Campeyyako mahiddhiko
tadâpi dhammiko âsi sîlabbatasamappito.
2 Tadâpi maṃ dhammacâriṃ upavuṭṭhaṃ uposathaṃ
ahikuṇḍiko gahetvâna râjadvâramhi kîḷati.
3 Yaṃ so vaṇṇaṃ cintayati nîlapîtaṃ va lohitaṃ
tassa cittânuvattanto homi cintitasannibho.

4 Thalaṃ kareyyam udakaṃ udakam pi thalaṃ kare.
yadi 'ham tassa pakuppeyaṃ khaṇena chârikaṃ kare.
5 Yadi cittavasî hessaṃ parihâyissâmi sîlato
sîlena parihînassa uttamattho na sijjhati.
6 Kâmaṃ bhijjatu yaṃ kâyo idh' eva vikirîyatu
n' eva sîlaṃ pabhindeyyaṃ vikirante bhusaṃ viyâ ti.

CAMPEYYANÂGACARIYAṂ TATIYAṂ.

IV.

THE STORY OF CÛLABODHI.

1 Punâparaṃ yadâ homi Cûlabodhi susîlavâ
bhavaṃ disvâna bhayato nekkhammaṃ abhinikkhamiṃ.
2 Yâ me dutiyikâ âsi brâhmaṇî kanakasannibhâ
sâ vivaṭṭe anapekhhâ nekkhammaṃ abhinikkhami.
3 Nirâlayâ chinnabhandû anapekkhâ kule gaṇe
carantâ gâmanigamaṃ Bârâṇasim upâgamuṃ.
4 Tattha vasâma nipakâ asaṃsaṭṭhâ kule gaṇe
nirâkule appasadde râj' uyyâne vasâm' ubho.
5 Uyyânadassanaṃ gantvâ râjâ addasa brâhmaṇiṃ
upagamma mamaṃ pucchi tuyh' esâ kassa bhariyâ ti?
6 Evaṃ vutte ahaṃ tassa idaṃ vacanam abraviṃ:
na mayhaṃ bhariyâ esâ sahadhammâ ekasâsanî.
7 Tassâ sârattâdhigato gâhâpetvâna cetake
nippîḷayanto balasâ antepuraṃ pavesayi.
8 Odapattikiyâ mayhaṃ sahajâ ekasâsanî
âkaḍḍhitvâ niyantiyâ kopo me upapajjatha.
9 Saha kope samuppanne sîlabbatam anussariṃ
tatth' eva kopaṃ niggaṇhiṃ nâdâsi vuḍḍhitum pari.
10 Yadi naṃ brâhmaṇiṃ koci koṭṭeyya tiṇhasattiyâ
n' eva sîlaṃ pabhindeyyaṃ bodhiyâ yeva kâraṇâ.
11 Na me sâ brâhmaṇî dessâ na pi me balaṃ na vijjati
sabbaññutam piyaṃ mayhaṃ tasmâ sîlânurakkhissan ti.

CÛLABODHICARIYAṂ CATUTTHAṂ.

V.

THE STORY OF THE BUFFALO-KING.

1 Punâparaṃ yadâ homi mahiṃso vanacârako
pavaḍḍhakâyo balavâ mahanto bhîmadassano
2 Pabbhâre giridugge ca rukkhamûle dakâsaye
hot' ettha ṭhânaṃ mahiṃsânaṃ koci koci tahiṃ tahiṃ.
3 Vicaranto brahâraññe ṭhânaṃ addasa bhaddakaṃ
taṃ ṭhânaṃ upagantvâna tiṭṭhâmi ca sayâmi ca.
4 Ath' ettha kapi mâgantvâ pâpo anariyo lahu
khande nalâṭe bhamuke mutteti ohaneti taṃ.
5 Sakim pi divasaṃ dutiyaṃ tatiyaṃ catuttham pi ca
dûseti maṃ sabbakâlaṃ tena homi upadduto.
6 Mamaṃ upaddutaṃ disvâ yakkho maṃ idam abravi:—
nâseh' etaṃ chavaṃ pâpaṃ siṅgehi ca khurehi ca.
7 Evaṃ vutte tadâ yakkhe ahaṃ taṃ idam abraviṃ:—
kiṃ tvaṃ makkhesi kuṇapena pâpena anariyena maṃ?
8 Yadi 'haṃ tassa kuppeyyaṃ tato hînataro bhave
sîlañ ca me pabhijjeyya viññû ca gahareyyuṃ maṃ.
9 Hîḷitâ jîvitâ vâpi parisuddhena mataṃ varaṃ
kyâhaṃ jîvitahetu pi kâhâmi paraheṭhanaṃ.
10 Maṃ evâyaṃ maññamâno aññe p' evaṃ karissati
te va tattha vadhissanti sâ me mutti bhavissati.
11 Hînamajjhimaukkaṭṭhe sahanto avamânitaṃ
evaṃ labhati sappañño manasâ yathâ patthitan ti.

MAHIṂSARÂJACARIYAṂ PAÑCAMAṂ.

VI.

THE STORY OF THE RURU-DEER.

1 Punâparaṃ yadâ homi suttattakanakasannibho
Migarâjâ Ruru nâma paramasîlasamâhito
2 Ramme padese rammaṇîye vivitte amanussake
tattha vâsaṃ upagañchiṃ Gaṅgâkûle manorame.

3 Atha upari Gaṅgâya dhanikehi paripîḷito
puriso Gangâya patati jîvâmi vâ marâmi vâ.
4 Rattiṃ divaṃ so Gaṅgâya vuyhamâno mahodake
ravanto karuṇaṃ ravaṃ majjhe Gaṅgâya gacchàti.
5 Tassâhaṃ saddaṃ sutvâna karuṇaṃ paridevato
Gaṅgâya tîre ṭhatvâna apucchiṃ ko si tvaṃ naro?
6 So me puṭṭho ca vyâkâsi attano kâraṇaṃ tadâ.
dhanikehi bhîto tasito pakkhanto 'haṃ mahânadiṃ.
7 Tassa katvâna kâruññañ cajitvâ mama jîvitaṃ
pavisitvâ nîharin tassa andhakârambhi rattiyâ.
8 Assattha kâlam aññâya tassâhaṃ idam abraviṃ :—
ekan taṃ varaṃ yâcâmi mâ maṃ kassaci pâvada.
9 Nagaraṃ gantvâna âcikkhi pucchito dhanahetuko
râjânaṃ so gahetvâna upagañchi mam' antikaṃ.
10 Yâvatâ kâraṇaṃ sabbaṃ rañño ârocitaṃ mayâ
râjâ sutvâna vacanaṃ ussuṃ tassa vikappayi :—
idh' eva ghâṭayissâmi mittadubbhim anariyaṃ.
11 Tam ahaṃ anurakkhanto nimmini mama attanâ :—
tiṭṭha te so mahârâja kâmaṅkâro bhavâmi te.
12 Anurakkhiṃ mama sîlaṃ nârakkhiṃ mama jîvitaṃ
sîlavâ hi tadâ âsiṃ bodhiyâ yeva kâraṇâ ti.

RURURÂJACARIYAṂ CHAṬṬHAMAṂ.

VII.

THE STORY OF MÂTAṄGA.

1 Punâparaṃ yadâ homi jaṭilo uggatâpano
Mâtaṅgo nâma nâmena sîlavâ susamâhito.
2 Ahañ ca brâhmaṇo eko Gaṅgâkûle vasâm' ubho
ahaṃ vasâmi upari heṭṭhâ vasati brâhmaṇo.
3 Vicaranto anukûlamhi uddham me assam' addasa
tattha maṃ paribhâsetvâ abhisapi muddhaphâlanaṃ.
4 Yadi 'haṃ tassa kuppeyyaṃ yadi sîlaṃ na gopaye
oloketvân' ahan tassa kareyyaṃ chârikaṃ viya.

5 Yaṃ so tadâ mam abhisapi kupito duṭṭhamânaso
tass' eva matthake nipati yogena taṃ pamocayiṃ.
6 Anurakkhiṃ mama sîlaṃ nârakkhiṃ mama jîvitaṃ
sîlavâ hi tadâ âsiṃ bodhiyâ yeva kâraṇâ ti.

MÂTAṄGACARIYAṂ SATTAMAṂ.

VIII.

THE STORY OF THE JUST YAKKHA.

1 Punâparaṃ yadâ homi mahâyakkho mahiddhiko
Dhammo nâma mahâyakkho sabbalokânukampako.
2 Dasakusalakammapathe samâdapento mahâjanaṃ
Carâmi gâmanigamaṃ samitto saparijjano.
3 Pâpo kadariyo yakkho dîpento dasa pâvake
So p' ettha mahiyâ carati samitto saparijjano.
4 Dhammavâdî Adhammo ca ubho paccanikâ mayaṃ
dhure dhuraṃ ghaṭṭayantâ samimhâ paṭipathe ubho.
5 Kalaho vattati asmâ kalyâṇapâpakassa ca
maggâ okkamanatthâya mahâyuddho upaṭṭhito.
6 Yadi 'haṃ tassa pakuppeyyaṃ yadi bhinde tapoguṇaṃ
saha parijanan tassa rajabhûtaṃ kareyy' ahaṃ.
7 Api câhaṃ sîla rakkhâya nibbâpetvâna mânasaṃ
saha janen' okkamitvâ pathaṃ pâpass' adâs' ahaṃ.
8 Saha pathato okkanto katvâ cittassa nibbutiṃ
vivaraṃ adâsi paṭhavî pâpayakkhassa tâvade ti.

DHAMMÂDHAMMADEVAPUTTACARIYAṂ AṬṬHAMAṂ.

IX.

THE STORY OF JAYADDISA.

1 Pañcâlaraṭṭhe nagare Kappilâyaṃ puruttame
râjâ Jayaddiso nâma sîlaguṇam upâgato.
2 Tassa rañño ahaṃ putto Sutadhammo susîlavâ
alînasatto guṇavâ anuttaraparijjano sadâ.
3 Pitâ me migavaṃ gantvâ porisâdam upâgami
so me pitum aggahesi bakkho si mama mâ cali.
4 Tassa taṃ vacanaṃ sutvâ bhîto tasitavedhito
uruthambho ahu tassa disvâna porisâdakaṃ.
5 Migavaṃ gahetvâ muñcassu katvâ âgamanaṃ puna.
brâhmaṇassa dhanaṃ datvâ pitâ âmantayi mamaṃ.
6 Rajjaṃ putta paṭipajja mâ pamajji puraṃ idaṃ
kataṃ me porisâdena mama âgamanaṃ puna.
7 Mâtâ pitu ca vanditvâ niminitvâna attânaṃ
nikkhipetvâ dhanukhaggaṃ porisâdaṃ upâgamiṃ.
8 Sasatthahatthûpagataṃ kadâci so tasissati
tena bhijjissati sîlaṃ parittâsaṃ kate mayi.
9 Sîlakhaṇḍabhayâ mayhaṃ tassa dessaṃ na vyâhariṃ
mettacitto hitavâdî idaṃ vacanam abraviṃ:—
10 Ujjalehi mahâ aggiṃ papatissâmi rukkhato
sampattakâlam aññâya bhakkhaya tvaṃ pitâmaha.
11 Iti sîlavataṃ hetu nârakkhiṃ mama jîvitaṃ
pabbâjesiñ câhaṃ tassa sadâ pâṇâtipâtikan ti.

JAYADDISACARIYAṂ NAVAMAṂ.

X.

THE STORY OF SAṄKHAPÂLA.

1 Punâparaṃ yadâ homi Saṅkhapâlo mahiddhiko
dâṭhâvudho ghoraviso dvijivho uragâdhibhû.
2 Catupathe mahâmagge nânâjanasamâkule
caturo aṅge adhiṭṭhâya tattha vâsâm akappayiṃ.
3 Chaviyâ cammena maṃsena nahâru-aṭṭhikehi vâ
yassa etena karaṇîyaṃ dinnaṃ yeva harâtu so.
4 Addasaṃsu bhojaputtâ kharâ luddâ akâruṇâ
upagañchuṃ mamaṃ tattha daṇḍamuggarapâṇino.
5 Nâsâya vinivijjhitvâ naṅguṭṭhe piṭṭhikaṇṭake
kâje âropayitvâna bhojaputtâ hariṃsu maṃ.
6 Sasâgaran taṃ paṭhaviṃ sakânanaṃ sapabbataṃ
icchamâno c' ahaṃ tattha nâsavâtena jhâpaye.
7 Sûlehi vijjhayante pi koṭṭayante pi sattibhi.
bhojaputte na kuppâmi esâ me sîlapâramî ti.

SAṄKHAPÂLACARIYAṂ DASAMAṂ.

8 Hatthinâgo, Bhûridatto, Campeyyo, Bodhimâhiso,
Ruru, Mâtaṅgo, Dhammo ca atrajo ca Jayaddiso.
9 Ete sabbe sîlabalâ parikkhârâ padesikâ
jîvitaṃ parikkhitvâ sîlâni anurakkhissaṃ.
10 Saṅkhapâlassa me sato sabbakâlam pi jîvitaṃ
Yassa kassaci nîyantaṃ tasmâ sâ sîlapâramî ti.

SÎLAPÂRAMI-NIDDESO NIṬṬHITO.

Book III.

NEKKHAMMAPÂRAMITA, &c.

I.

THE STORY OF YUDHAÑJAYA.

1 Yadâ ahaṃ amitayaso râjaputto Yudhañjayo
ussâvabinduṃ suriyâtape patitaṃ disvâna saṃviji
2 Tañ ñevâdhipatikatvâ saṃvegam anubrûhayiṃ.
mâtâ pitu ca vanditvâ pabbajjam anuyâc' ahaṃ.
3 Yâcanti maṃ pañjalikâ sanegamâ saraṭṭhakâ
ajj' eva putta paṭipajja iddhaṃ phîtaṃ mahâmahiṃ.
4 Sarâjake sah' orodhe sanegame saraṭṭhake
karuṇaṃ paridevante anapekkho hi pabbajiṃ.
5 Kevalaṃ paṭhavi-rajjaṃ ñâtiparijanaṃ yasaṃ
cajamâno na cintesiṃ bodhiyâ yeva kâraṇâ.
6 Mâtâ pitâ na me dessâ na pi dessaṃ mahâyasaṃ
sabbaññutam piyaṃ mayhaṃ tasmâ rajjaṃ pariccajin ti.

YUDHAÑJAYACARIYAṂ PAṬHAMAṂ.

II.

THE STORY OF SOMANASSA.

1 Punâparaṃ yadâ homi Inda-patthe puruttame
kâmito dayito putto Somanasso ti vissuto.
2 Sîlavâ guṇasampanno kalyâṇapaṭibhânavâ
vuḍḍhâpacâyî hirimâ saṅgahesu ca kovido.
3 Tassa rañño patikaro âsi kuhakatâpaso
ârâmaṃ mâlâvacchañ ca ropitvâna so jîvati.

4 Tam ahaṃ disvâna kuhakaṃ thusarâsiṃ va ataṇḍulaṃ
dumaṃ anto ca susiraṃ kadaliṃ va asârakaṃ
5 N' atthi m' assasataṃ dhammo sâmaññâpagato ayaṃ
hirisukkadhammajahito jîvitavuttikâraṇâ.
6 Kupito ahosi paccanto aṭavîhi parantihi
taṃ nisedhetuṃ gacchanto anusâsi pitâ mamaṃ.
7 Mâ pamajji tuvaṃ tâta jaṭilaṃ uggatâpanaṃ
yadicchakaṃ pavattehi sabbakâmadado hi so.
8 Tam ahaṃ gantvân' upaṭṭhânaṃ idaṃ vacanam abraviṃ:—
kacci te gahapati kusalaṃ kiṃ vâ te âhariyyatu?
9 Tena so kupito âsi kuhako mânanissitô
ghâṭâpemi tuvaṃ ajja raṭṭhâ pabbâjayâmi vâ.
10 Nisedhayitvâ paccantaṃ râjâ kuhakam abravi:—
kacci te bhante khamanîyaṃ sammâno te pavattito?
tassa âcikkhati pâpo kumâro yathâ nâsito
11 Tassa taṃ vacanaṃ sutvâ âṇâpesi mahîpati.
sîsaṃ tatth' eva chinditvâ katvâna catukhaṇḍikaṃ
rathiyâ rathiyaṃ dassetha sâ gatijaṭilahîḷitâ.
12 Tatth' akâruṇikâ gantvâ caṇḍâ luddâ akâruṇâ
mâtu aṅke nisinnassa âkaḍḍhitvan' ayanti maṃ.
13 Tesâhaṃ evam avacaṃ:—bandha taṃ gâḷhabandhanaṃ
rañño dassetha maṃ khippaṃ râjakiriyâni atthi me.
14 Te maṃ rañño dassayiṃsu pâpassa pâpasevino
disvâna taṃ saññâpesiṃ mamañ ca vasam âṇayiṃ
15 So maṃ tattha khamâpesi mahârajjam adâsi me
so' haṃ tamaṃ dâlayetvâ pabbajiṃ anagâriyaṃ.
16 Na me dessaṃ mahârajjaṃ kâmabhogo na dessiyo
sabbaññutam piyaṃ mayhaṃ tasmâ rajjaṃ pariccajin ti.

SOMANASSACARIYAṂ DUTIYAṂ.

III.

THE STORY OF AYOGHARA.

1 Punâparaṃ yadâ homi Kâsirâjassa atrajo
Ayogharamhi saṃvaḍḍho nâmen' âsi Ayogharo.
2 Dukkhena jîviko laddho sampîḷe pati posito
ajj' eva putta paṭipajja kevalaṃ vasudhaṃ imaṃ.
3 Saraṭṭhakaṃ sanigamaṃ sajanaṃ vanditvâ khattiyaṃ
añjaliṃ paggahetvâna idaṃ vacanam abravi :—
4 Ye keci mahiyâ sattâ hînamukkaṭṭhamajjhimâ
nirârakkhâ sake gehe vaḍḍhanti saha ñâtibhi.
5 Idaṃ loke uttariyaṃ sampîḷe mama posanaṃ
Ayogharamhi saṃvaḍḍho appabhe candasuriye.
6 Pûtikuṇapasampuṇṇâ muccitvâ mâtu kucchito
tato ghoratare dukkhe puna pakkhitt' Ayoghare.
7 Yadi 'haṃ tâdisam patvâ dukkhaṃ paramadâruṇaṃ
rajjesu yadi rajjâmi pâpânam uttamo siyaṃ.
8 Ukkaṇṭhito 'mhi kâyena rajjena 'mhi anatthiko
nibbutiṃ pariyesissaṃ yattha maṃ maccu na maddiye.
9 Evâham cintayitvâna viravantaṃ mahâjanaṃ
nâgo va bandhanaṃ chetvâ pâvisi kânanaṃ vanaṃ.
10 Mâtâ pitâ na me dessâ na pi me dessaṃ mahâyasaṃ
sabbaññutam piyaṃ mayhaṃ tasmâ rajjaṃ pariccajin ti.

AYOGHARACARIYAṂ TATIYAṂ.

IV.

THE STORY OF BHISA.

1 Punâparaṃ yadâ homi Kâsinaṃ puravaruttame
bhaginî bhâtaro satta nibbattâ sotthiye kule.
2 Etesaṃ pubbajo âsiṃ hirisukkam upâgato
bhavaṃ disvâna bhayato nekkhammâbhirato ahaṃ.

3 Mâtâ-pitûhi pahitâ sahâyâ ekamânasâ
kâmehi maṃ nimantenti kulavaṃsaṃ dharehî ti.
4 Yaṃ tesaṃ vacanaṃ vuttaṃ gihîdhamme sukhâvahaṃ
taṃ me ahosi kaṭhinaṃ tattaphâlasamaṃ viya.
5 Te maṃ tadâ ukkhipantaṃ pucchiṃsu patthitaṃ mama
kiṃ tvaṃ patthayasi samma yadi kâme na bhuñjasi?
6 Tesâhaṃ evaṃ avacaṃ atthakâmo hitesinaṃ
nâhaṃ patthemi gihîbhâvaṃ nekkhammâbhirato ahaṃ.
7 Te mayhaṃ vacanaṃ sutvâ pitu mâtu ca sâveyyuṃ
mâtâ pitâ evam âhu: sabbe pi pabbajjâma bho.
8 Ubho mâtâ pitâ mayhaṃ bhaginî ca satta bhâtaro.
amitadhanaṃ chaḍḍayitvâ pâvisimhâ mahâvanan ti.

BHISACARIYAṂ CATUTTHAṂ.

V.

THE STORY OF SOṆA.

1 Punâparaṃ yadâ homi nagare Brahmavaḍḍhane
tattha kulavare seṭṭhe mahâsâle ajây' ahaṃ.
2 Tadâpi lokaṃ disvâna andhabhûtaṃ tamotthataṃ
cittaṃ bhavato paṭikuṭati tuttavegahataṃ viya.
3 Disvâna vividhaṃ pâpaṃ evaṃ cintes' ahaṃ tadâ
kadâhaṃ gehâ nikkhamma pavisissâmi kânanaṃ.
4 Tadâpi maṃ nimantiṃsu kâmabhogehi ñâtayo
tesam pi chandam âcikkhi mâ nimantetha tehi maṃ.
5 Yo me kaniṭṭhako bhâtâ Nando nâmâsi paṇḍito
so pi maṃ anusikkhanto pabbajjaṃ samarocayi.
6 Ahaṃ Soṇo ca Nando ca ubho mâtâ pitâ mama
tadâpi bhoge chaḍḍetvâ pâvisimhâ mahâvanan ti.

SOṆAPAṆḌITACARIYAṂ PAÑCAMAṂ.

VI.

THE STORY OF TEMIYA.

1 Punâparaṃ yadâ homi Kâsirâjassa atrajo
Mûgapakkho ti nâmena Temiyo ti vadanti maṃ.
2 Soḷasitthisahassânaṃ na vijjati pumo tadâ
ahorattânaṃ accayena nibbatto aham ekako.
3 Kicchâ laddhâm piyaṃ puttaṃ abhijâtaṃ jutindharaṃ
setacchattaṃ dhârayitvâna sayane poseti maṃ pitâ.
4 Niddâyamâno sayanavare pabujjhitvân' ahaṃ tadâ
addasaṃ paṇḍaraṃ chattaṃ yenâhaṃ nirayaṅgato.
5 Saha diṭṭhassa me chattaṃ tâso uppajji bheravo
vinicchayaṃ samâpanno kadâhaṃ imaṃ muccissaṃ.
6 Pubbasâlohitâ mayhaṃ devatâ atthakâminî
sâ maṃ disvâna dukkhitaṃ tîsu ṭhânesu yojayi.
7 Mâ paṇḍiccaṃ vibhâvaya bahumataṃ sappâṇinaṃ
sabbo jano ocinâyatu evaṃ attho bhavissati.
8 Evaṃ vuttây' ahaṃ tassâ idaṃ vacanam abravi :—
karomi te taṃ vacanaṃ yaṃ tvaṃ bhaṇasi devate
9 Atthakâmâ si me amma hitakâmâ si devate.
tassâhaṃ vacanaṃ sutvâ sâgare va thalaṃ labhiṃ
10 Haṭṭho saṃviggamânaso tayo aṅge adhiṭṭhahiṃ.
mûgo ahosiṃ badhiro pakkho gativivajjito.
11 Ete aṅge adhiṭṭhâya vassânaṃ soḷasaṃ vasi.
tato me hatthapâde ca jivhaṃ sotañ ca maddiya
anûnataṃ me passitvâ Kâḷakaṇṇî ti nindiṃsuṃ.
12 Tato janapadâ sabbe senâpatipurohitâ
sabbe ekamanâ hutvâ chaḍḍanaṃ anumodiṃsuṃ.
13 So 'haṃ tesaṃ matiṃ sutvâ haṭṭho saṃviggamânaso
yassatthâya tapo ciṇṇo so me attho samijjhatha.
14 Nhâpetvâ anulimpitvâ veṭhetvâ râjaveṭhanaṃ
chattena abhisiñcitvâ kâresuṃ purapadakkhiṇaṃ.
15 Sattâhaṃ dhârayitvâna uggate ravimaṇḍale
rathena maṃ nîharitvâ sârathî vanam upâgami.

16 Ek' okâse ratham katvâ sajjassam hatthamuñcitam
sârathi khaṇati kâsum nikhâtum paṭhaviyâ mamam.
17 Adhiṭṭhitam adhiṭṭhânam tajjanto vividhakâraṇâ
na bhindi va tam adhiṭṭhânam bodhiyâ yeva kâraṇâ.
18 Matâ pitâ na me dessâ attâ na me ca dessiyo
sabbaññutam piyam mayham tasmâ va tam adhiṭṭhahim.
19 Ete aṅge adhiṭṭhâya vassâni solasam vasim.
adhiṭṭhânena samo n' atthi esâ me adhiṭṭhânapâramî ti.

TEMIYACARIYAṂ CHAṬṬHAMAṂ.

VII.

THE STORY OF THE MONKEY-KING.

1 Yadâ aham kapi âsim nadîkûle darîsaye
pîḷito samsumârena gamanam na labhâmi 'ham.
2 Yamh' okâse aham ṭhatvâ orapâram patâm' aham
tatth' acchi satthu vadhako kumbhilo ruddadassano.
3 So mam asamsi ehî ti : aham emî ti tam vadi
tassa matthakam akkamma parakûle patiṭṭhahim
4 Na tassa alikam bhaṇitam yathâ vâcam akâs' aham.
saccena me samo n' atthi esâ me saccapâramî ti.

KAPIRÂJACARIYAṂ PATTAMAṂ.

VIII.

THE STORY OF SACCA.

1 Punâparam yadâ homi tâpaso Saccasavhayo
saccena lokam pâlesim samaggam janam akâs' ahan ti.

SACCASAVHAYAPAṆḌITACARIYAṂ AṬṬHAMAṂ.

IX.

THE STORY OF THE YOUNG QUAIL.

1 Punâparaṃ yadâ homi Magadhe vaṭṭapotako
ajâtapakkho taruṇo maṃsapesi kulâvake
2 Mukhatuṇḍaken' âharitvâ mâtâ posayati mamaṃ
tassâ phassena jîvâmi n' atthi me kâyikaṃ balaṃ.
3 Saṃvacchare gimhasamaye davaḍâho padippati
upagacchati ambâkaṃ pâvako kaṇhavattanî.
4 Dhûmadhûmañ janitv' evaṃ saddâyanto mahâ sikhî
anupubbena jhâpento aggi mamam upâgami.
5 Aggivegabhayâ bhîtâ tasitâ mâtâ pitâ mama
kulâvake maṃ chaḍḍetvâ attânaṃ parimocayuṃ.
6 Pâde pakkhe pajahâmi n' atthi me kâyikaṃ balaṃ
so 'haṃ agatiko tattha evaṃ cintes' ahaṃ tadâ.
7 Yesâhaṃ upadhâveyyaṃ bhîto tasitavedhito
te maṃ ohâya pakkantâ kathaṃ me ajja kâtave.
8 Atthi loke sîlaguṇo saccaṃ soceyy' anuddayâ
tena saccena kâhâmi saccakiriyam uttamaṃ.
9 Âvajjetvâ dhammabalaṃ saritvâ pubbake jine
saccabalam avassâya saccakiriyam akâs' ahaṃ.
10 Santi pakkhâ apatanâ santi pâdâ avañcanâ
mâtâ pitâ ca nikkhantâ jâtavedapaṭikkama.
11 Saha sacce kate mayhaṃ mahâpajjaliko sikhî
vajjesi soḷasakarîsâni udakaṃ patvâ yathâ sikhî.
saccena me samo n' atthi esâ me saccapâramî ti.

VAṬṬAPOTAKACARIYAṂ NAVAMAṂ.

X.

THE STORY OF THE FISH-KING.

1 Punâparaṃ yadâ homi maccharâjâ mahâsare
unhe suriyasantâpe sare udakaṃ khîyatha.
2 Tato kâkâ ca gijjhâ ca bakâ kulalasenakâ
bhakkhayanti divâ rattiṃ macche upanisîdiya.
3 Evaṃ cintes' ahaṃ tattha saha ñâtîhi pîḷito
kena nu kho upâyena ñâtî dukkhâ pamocaye?
4 Vicintayitvâ dhammatthaṃ saccaṃ addasa passayaṃ
sacce ṭhatvâ pamocesiṃ ñâtînaṃ taṃ atikkhayaṃ.
5 Anussaritvâ saddhammaṃ paramatthaṃ vicintayaṃ
âkâsiṃ saccakiriyaṃ yaṃ loke dhuvasassataṃ.
6 Yato sarâmi attânaṃ yato patto 'smi viññutaṃ
nâbhijânâmi sañcicca ekam pâṇaṃ vihiṃsitaṃ
etena saccavajjena pajjunno abhivassatu.
7 Abhitthanaya pajjunna nidhiṃ kâkassa nâsaya
kâkaṃ sokâya rundhehi macche sokâ pamocaya.
8 Saha kate saccavare pajjunno o' abhigajjiya
thalaṃ ninnañ ca pûrento khaṇena abhivassatha.
9 Evarûpaṃ saccavaraṃ katvâ viriyam uttamaṃ
vassâpesiṃ mahâmeghaṃ saccatejabalassito.
saccena me samo n' atthi esâ me saccapâramî ti.

MACCHARÂJACARIYAṂ DASAMAṂ.

XI.

THE STORY OF KAṆHADIPÂYANO.

1 Punâparaṃ yadâ homi Kaṇha-dîpâyano isi
paro paññâsavassâni anabhirato cariṃ ahaṃ.
2 Na koci etaṃ jânâti anabhiratimanaṃ mama
aham pi kassaci nâcikkhim aratiṃ me ratimânase.

3 Sabrahmacârî Maṇḍabyo sahâyo me mahâ isi
pubbakammasamâyutto sûlamâropanaṃ labbi.
4 Tam ahaṃ upaṭṭhahitvâna ârogyam anupâpayi.
âpucchitvâna âgañchi yaṃ mayhaṃ sakam assamaṃ.
5 Sahâyo brâhmaṇo mayhaṃ bhariyam âdâya puttakaṃ
tayo janâ samâgantvâ âgañchuṃ pâhunâgataṃ.
6 Sammodamâno tehi saha nisinno sakamassame
dârako vaṭṭam anukkhipam âsîvisam akopayi.
7 Tato so vaṭṭagataṃ maggaṃ anvesanto kumârako
âsîvisassa hathena uttamaṅgaṃ parâmasi.
8 Tassa âmasane kuddho sappo visabalassito
kupito paramakopena aḍaṃsi dârakaṃ khaṇe.
9 Saha daṭṭho ativisena dârako patati bhûmiyaṃ
tenâhaṃ dukkhito âsiṃ mama vâ hasitaṃ dukkhaṃ.
10 Tyâhaṃ assâsayitvâna dukkhite sokasallite
paṭhamaṃ akâsi kiriyaṃ aggaṃ saccaṃ varuttamaṃ.
11 Sattâham evâhaṃ pasannacitto
puññatthiko acarî brahmacariyaṃ
athâparaṃ yaṃ caritaṃ mama yidaṃ
vassâni paññâsasamâdhikâni.
12 Akâmako vâhi ahaṃ carâmi
etena saccena suvatthi hotu
hataṃ visaṃ jîvatu Yaññadatto.
13 Saha sacce kate mayhaṃ visavegena vedhito
abujjhitvâna vuṭṭhâsi ârogo câsi mâṇavo.
saccena me samo n' atthi esâ me saccapâramî ti.

KAṆHADÎPÂYANACARIYAṂ EKÂDASAMAṂ.

XII.

THE STORY OF SUTASOMA.

1 Punâparaṃ yadâ homi Sutasomo mahîpati
gahito porisâdena brâhmaṇe saṅkaraṃ sariṃ.
2 Khattiyânaṃ ekasataṃ âvunitvâ karatale
ete sampamilâpetvâ yaññatthe upanayi mamaṃ.

3 Apucchi maṃ porisâdo kiṃ tvaṃ icchasi nissajjaṃ?
yathâ mati te kâhâmi yadi me tvaṃ pun' ehisi.
4 Tassa paṭisuṇitvâna paṇhe âgamanaṃ mama
upagantvâ puraṃ rammaṃ rajjaṃ nîyyâdayiṃ tadâ.
5 Anussaritvâ sataṃ dhammaṃ pubbakaṃ jinasevitaṃ
brâhmaṇassa dhanaṃ datvâ porisâdaṃ upâgamiṃ.
6 N' atthi me saṃsayo tattha ghâtayissati vâ na vâ
saccavâcânurakkhanto jîvitañ cajitum upâgami.
saccena me samo n' atthi esâ me saccapâramî ti.

SUTASOMACARIYAṂ DVÂDASAMAṂ.

XIII.

THE STORY OF SUVAṆṆA-SÂMA.

1 Sâmo yadâ vane âsiṃ Sakkena abhinimmito.
pavane sîhavyagghe ca mettâyam upanâmayiṃ.
2 Sîhavyagghehi dîpehi acchehi mahisehi ca
pasadamigavarâhehi parivâretvâ vane vasiṃ.
3 Na maṃ koci uttassati na pi bhâyâmi kassaci
mettâbalen' upatthaddho ramâmi pavane tadâ ti.

SUVAṆṆASÂMACARIYAṂ.

XIV.

THE HISTORY OF EKARÂJÂ.

1 Punâparaṃ yadâ homi Ekarâjâ ti vissuto
paramaṃ sîlam adhiṭṭhâya pasâsâmi mahâmahiṃ.
2 Dasakusalakammapathe vattâmi anavasesato
catûhi saṅgahavatthûhi saṅgaṇhâmi mahâjanaṃ.
3 Evaṃ me appamattassa idha loke parattha ca

Dabbaseno upâgantvâ acchindanto puraṃ mamaṃ.
4 Râjûpajîve nigame sabalaṭṭhe saraṭṭhake
sabbaṃ hatthagataṃ katvâ kâsuyâ nikkhani mamaṃ.
5 Amaccamaṇḍalaṃ rajjaṃ phîtam antepuraṃ mama
acchinditvâna gahitaṃ piyaṃ puttaṃ va pass' ahaṃ.
mettâya me samo n' atthi esa me mettâparâmî ti.

EKARÂJACARIYAṂ CUDDASAMAṂ.

XV.

THE STORY OF THE GREAT REJOICING.

1 Susâne seyyaṃ kappemi chavaṭṭhikaṃ nidhây' ahaṃ
gâmaṇḍalâ upagantvâ rûpaṃ dassenti 'nappakaṃ.
2 Apare gandhañ ca mâlañ ca bhojanaṃ vividhaṃ bahuṃ
upâyanâny' upanenti haṭṭhâ saṃviggamânasâ.
3 Ye me dukkhaṃ upadahanti ye ca denti sukhaṃ mama
sabbesaṃ samako homi dayakopo na vijjati.
4 Sukhadukkhe tulâbhûto yasesu ayasesu ca
sabbattha samako homi esâ me upekkhâpâramî ti.

MAHÂLOMAHAṂSACARIYAṂ PAṆṆARASAMAṂ.

5 Yudhañjayo, Somanasso, Ayogharabhisena ca,
Soṇanando, Mûgapakkho, Kapirâjâ, Saccasavhayo,
6 Vaṭṭako, Maccharâjâ ca, Kaṇha-dîpâyano isi,
Sutasomo puna âsiṃ Sâmo ca Ekarâj' ahu
Upekkhâparâmî âsi itivuttaṃ mahesinâ.
7 Evaṃ bahuvidhaṃ dukkhaṃ sampatti ca bahûvidhâ
bhavâbhave anubhavitvâ patto sambodhim uttamaṃ.
8 Datvâ dâtabbakaṃ dânaṃ sîlaṃ pûretvâ asesato
nikkhamme pâramiṃ gantvâ patto sambodhim uttamaṃ.
9 Paṇḍite paripucchitvâ viriyaṃ katvânam uttamaṃ
khantiyâ pâramiṃ gantvâ patto sambodhim uttamaṃ.
10 Katvâ daḷham adhiṭṭhânaṃ saccavâcânurakkhiya

mettâya pâramiṃ gantvâ patto sambodhim uttamaṃ.
11 Lâbhâlâbhe yasâyase samânanâvamânane
sabbattha samâno hutvâ patto sambodhim uttamaṃ.
12 Kosajjaṃ bhayato disvâ viriyârambhaṃ ca khemato
âraddhaviriyâ hotha esâ buddhânusâsanî.
13 Vivâdaṃ bhayato disvâ avivâdañ ca khemato
samaggâ akhilâ hotha esâ buddhânusâsanî.
14 Pamâdaṃ bhayato disvâ appamâdañ ca khemato
bhâve atthaṅgikaṃ maggaṃ esâ buddhânusâsanî.

Itthaṃ sudaṃ bhagavâ attano pubbacariyaṃ sambhâviyamâno Buddhâpadâni yan nâma dhammapariyâyam abhâsitthâ ti.

CARIYÂPIṬAKAṂ NIṬṬHITAṂ.

C. adds the following lines:—

Yasmâ pana ayaṃ pâḷi paramparâya likkhitâ
vipallaṭṭhakkharâ tasmâ sâyaṃ suṭṭhu visodhitâ
Paññâsîho ti nâmena anutherena dhîmatâ
sâsanaṭṭhitikâmena bahugandhesu âgataṃ
Atthaṃ saṃsanditvâ mayâ tassa tejena pânino
samiddhasaṅkappâ hontu devâ rakkhantu sâsanaṃ.

CARIYÂPIṬAKAPÂLI SAMATTÂ.